INTRUDERS ON THE RIGHTS OF MEN

Lynne Spender

Lynne Spender is an Australian feminist writer who has recently returned to Australia having lived for several years in North America where she researched and wrote this book. She combines the study of Law and the teaching of Women's Studies with the writing of a book about the myths and the reality of marriage for women.

Cover Illustration Christine Roche is a freelance cartoonist and illustrator. She is French Canadian and has been living and working in London since 1969.

INTRUDERS ON THE RIGHTS OF MEN

Women's Unpublished Heritage

Lynne Spender

PANDORA PRESS

Routledge & Kegan Paul
London, Boston, Melbourne and Henley

First published in 1983
by Pandora Press
(Routledge & Kegan Paul plc)
39 Store Street, London WC1E 7DD,
9 Park Street, Boston, Mass. 02108, USA,
296 Beaconsfield Parade, Middle Park,
Melbourne, 3206, Australia, and
Broadway House, Newtown Road,
Henley-on-Thames, Oxon RG9 1EN
Photoset in 10 on 11½ Century Schoolbook by
Kelly Typesetting Limited
Bradford-on-Avon, Wiltshire,
and printed in Great Britain by
St Edmundsbury Press, Bury St Edmunds, Suffolk

Library of Congress Cataloging in Publication Data

Spender, Lynne.

Intruders on the rights of men.
Bibliography: p.
Includes index.
1. Feminism. 2. Publishers and publishing.
3. Power (Social sciences) I. Title.
HQ1154.S63 1983   305.4'2   82–22251

ISBN 0–86358–000–9

Contents

Alas, a woman that attempts the pen
Such an intruder on the rights of men.
Anne Finch, Countess of Winchilsea
(1661-1720)

Acknowledgments

Political

The information and the sensibility in this book are a direct product of the knowledge and awareness created by the current women's movement. Without the committed work of many other feminists and the networks that feminism has created, this book could not have been written and would certainly not have been published.

Personal

I owe thanks to my family for their moral and financial support and their willingness to share child care – even when it involved travelling half way around the world. For the living example of justice and fair play that my parents have given, I am deeply appreciative. To my friend Jill, I owe many thanks for her unfailing help, both practical and emotional, and for her demonstration that sisterhood can indeed be powerful. To my biological sister Dale, I am forever grateful for her sense of humour, her sense of balance and her encouragement of these qualities in others. It is to acknowledge the stimulus, criticism and love that she has always offered, willingly and unconditionally, that this book has been written.

Introduction

In literate societies, there is a close association between *the printed word* and the exercise of *power*. Because so many administrative and organizational tasks are carried out in print and because print forms the basic currency of education and literature, those who are involved in the *selection* of information and ideas to be published have a great deal of power to name the knowledge that will emerge in print. Similarly, those who control the distribution of the printed word have considerable power to decide who will have access to it; those who participate in its evaluation have the power to determine what status it will acquire. Ultimately, these powers to decide what knowledge will be made available and how it will appear and be received, constitute a great deal of power *over* society and its members.

When any group united by politics or ideology in a non-Western society has all these powers we are quick to cry 'propaganda' and to criticize their printed words as partial and biased. In contrast, we consider the printed words that emerge from our society to be the product of freedom of speech and expression. We tend to assume that publishing here takes place on a rational basis. We believe that the powers associated with the printed word are not in the hand of any one group and that no one doctrine is being promoted at the expense of others. We even tolerate the idea that 'freedom of the press belongs to those who own it', because we regard the truths embodied in our published heritage as non-partisan and universal. We rarely see them in association with particular power structures.

Since the 1960s, however, and at various times over the last two hundred years, women have challenged the universality of those truths and have pointed out that the knowledge encoded in the printed word and in our published heritage is frequently not true for women. Such knowledge does not incorporate female experiences from a female point of view and does not value them. Instead, our published heritage consists of records of men's experiences and perceptions. Even the information about women is provided by men and, as Virginia Woolf tells us, by all sorts of men including those 'who have no apparent qualification save that they are not women' (Woolf, 1977a, p. 28). Women's own records of their lives are simply not included. Indeed, as the long and rich tradition of women's writing is being recovered, women are realizing that their perceptions, values and understandings have consistently been excluded from or edited out of the printed words that make up our cultural heritage. They have been relegated to what constitutes an *unpublished heritage* of women's words and truths.

Attempts to explain the disparity between our published and our unpublished heritage lead straight to the institution of publishing. There, behind the facade of rationality and integrity, the shaping of women's unpublished heritage can be traced. By promoting the myth of male supremacy through the devaluation of women and their words, and by promoting the myth of the neutrality of knowledge, publishers have managed to project men's truths as universal truths. Women's lives and truths have acquired only marginal status and significance.

Connections between the male-controlled publishing industry and women's exclusion from 'legitimate' cultural forms are more than mere social conventions. They have a political dimension in that they exemplify the arrangements whereby men appropriate power and use it to maintain their positions of dominance. Awareness of these connections invites us to ask whether there is really much difference between a non-Western society where members of a certain political persuasion control the production and dissemination of knowledge and a Western society where the same tasks are carried out by white, educated men who have been reared in a patriarchal tradition of male supremacy. Should not their particular perspectives and their vested interests in promoting some truths and dismissing others be equally open to the criticism of being *political* in nature?

In theory the answer must be yes, but in practice, such criticism has never become a topic of concern partly because the men who control publishing also decided what will be named and circulated as a topic. Through a purposefully established system, men are given the privilege of choosing the topics and issues that will be considered of fundamental concern to society. In order to protect themselves and the *status quo*, they choose not to examine women's issues from the perspective of women.

Publishing is an institution controlled by men: as in other institutions controlled by men it constitutes a male dictatorship and as in other dictatorships, the power can be used to put out propaganda that is in the interests of the rulers. Alternative – or subversive views – can readily be suppressed.

So, at the moment, in spite of almost two decades of feminism during which time a tremendous amount of women's knowledge has been resurrected, as well as generated, this women's knowledge has been stigmatized and marginalized. It is women's knowledge, at best, the quaint ideas of the unrepresentative few, and at worst, the heresies of those bent on destruction. It is not knowledge which men have taken on as central, as the legitimate knowledge of half of humanity, with as many rights to significance and acceptance as their own. While women's knowledge challenges men's, it has not (as yet) deprived men of their power base: there have been no substantial changes.

Yet change is really what feminism is about. Feminists do have a notion of a society that can afford to seek diversity and where different 'truths' can be valued, rather than ranked and stratified. We do have a concept of a culture where women exist on equal terms with men and where women's contributions are granted equal validity.

This book explores some of the changes that might help bring such a society into being. By considering data from the past and documenting evidence from women currently engaged in writing and publishing, it aims to deconstruct the myths and mystique associated with the publishing industry. By placing the relationship between *power* and *print* in a political context, the information in this book places women in a position to recognize some of the arrangements that have worked for so long against our movement towards autonomy and equality. Hopefully, it will also place women in a position where we will never again have to reconstruct our past before we can anticipate our future.

Chapter 1

Gatekeeping

The values which a society holds and the institutions it creates are not an accident. They reflect the conscious and unconscious choices made by people in power and positions of authority. The way of life – and the quality of life – is directly or indirectly determined by the decisions which are made within the circles of the powerful.

There is nothing new about this understanding; be it nuclear weapons or the availability of creches, the disproportionate unemployment of blacks or the location of a new airport that is the explicit issue, there is widespread recognition that it is but a few who make the choices, even though it may be the many who feel the consequences. So it would be reassuring to know that those who enjoyed the privilege of decison-making were a 'representative' group, holding a range of values and priorities and able to appreciate the significance of their actions for all who are affected by them. Sleep would come easily at night if we were to know that the vast range of decisions which were being made – and which would impinge on our lives in myriad ways – were being undertaken in a fair and neutral manner, and embodied the needs and aspirations of all members of society.

But this is not the case. There is no reassurance. Since we have been keeping records we know that only half of humanity (and a segment of that half) has had any influence in the decision-making circles. The only values and priorities that have been reflected are those of the male. In each generation a group of privileged men, on the basis of their own experience and with the endorsement of other men, has had the right to decree the social values. It is not just a matter of whether there will be peace or war, mines or conservation areas, football pitches or child-minding facilities, that has been decided by men, but the more subtle – and some would say more insidious – *scheme* of values which would have us believe that war, or mines, or football pitches are sound and sensible ways of organizing society. What is considered significant, sane and suitable at the most basic level in our ordering of experience, has been decreed – and built upon – for centuries by a small band of men who have found it easy to accept that their ways are the right ways.

From government to education, from science to religion, from medicine to the media, it has been men who have been in command and given the orders; they have made the policy decisions and put them into practice through the organizations and institutions which they, as the dominant group, control.

This means that our culture, which we have been encouraged to see as *human* culture, is nothing other than a product of the understanding and beliefs of the dominant group – men! Regardless of their position in a male-determined hierarchy, women have never contributed to the making of our society in equal numbers and on the same terms as men. Even if tomorrow women were to comprise half the politicians, or business executives, or priests or scientists, what we have to keep in mind is that they would be coming into a system which men have devised for themselves, in which the values and the rules of the dominant group are already decreed, and into which the 'newcomers' would have to fit. For women to contribute to our value system, our social ideology and view of the world, on the same terms as men, women would have to be free to decree at least half the rules . . . by which men would have to abide.

Because we have become aware of the extent to which women have been excluded from this process of forming our values and beliefs, and because we are beginning to appreciate the significance of this male monopoly, we are currently witnessing a demand for women to be included in the circle of the decision makers . . . so that our society reflects the consciousness of both sexes. Yet we cannot confine the demand to the presence of women in *equal numbers*; if women are not *admitted on the same terms as men*, then men will be able to retain their dominance.

Our culture at the moment, far from representing the sum total of human experience, reflects the experience of men. What does not make sense to the dominant group therefore does not make sense; what is not a priority – or a problem – for men, is therefore not a priority or a problem. The 'social reality' which we inhabit, the view of the world into which we have all been initiated as members of society and which we are obliged to affirm, is one which takes as its standards, the standards of white, educated men. There are no 'alternative' standards which allow for the values and priorities of those who are not white, or male, for example; there is only one standard and those who display any departure from it are defined as 'not up to standard'. Our culture, ostensibly neutral and the outcome of human effort and consciousness, in reality embodies and encodes the values of the dominant group who have produced it:

> What is there – spoken, sung, written, made emblematic
> in art – and treated as general, universal, unrelated to a
> particular position or a particular sex as its source and
> standpoint, is in fact partial, limited, located in a
> particular position and permeated by special interests
> and concerns. (Dorothy Smith, 1978; p. 283)

Not surprisingly there are many women who object to this arrangement. For over a decade (this time round) feminists have been setting out the implications – for both sexes – of a system of values and beliefs that promotes and applauds the interests of one half of humanity and denies and derides the interests of the other half. In doing so we have come to understand (as our foremothers did) that it is not a case of pointing out to men the error (and injustice) of their ways so that they can mend them, it is a case of depriving the dominant group of their power base. Many men do not want to give it up.

We have not been excluded by accident. The institutions that men have established have frequently been *based* on our exclusion and designed to create sexual inequality. In the eighteenth century, for example, men excluded women from education and were then able to argue that because women were not educated they could make no worthwhile contribution to the culture. In the nineteenth century men excluded women from the political arena and were then able to argue that because women had no head for politics, they could play no part in running society. We can see in the past how the institutions which men had set up for themselves were used to reinforce and maintain women's subordination. What we tend to forget is that the same process is at work in the present.

In 1969 Kate Millett introduced into the language the term 'sexual politics' to refer to 'power structured relationships, arrangements whereby one group of persons is controlled by another' (p. 23). She did us the service of alerting us – yet again, for women have perceived this before (see Spender, 1982b) – to the *purposeful* nature of the arrangements in our society, where men have assumed power and control and have used it to keep women, as a group, without resources, and without access to both the public and private worlds that men have traditionally – and conveniently – enjoyed.

In 1973 Mary Daly raised the same issue in another way when she recognized the power that goes with the ability to 'name the world' – to decree what is real, what is reasonable, what is right. Women have not had access to that power. Men have been the 'producers' of the belief system and women the 'consumers'. Men's way of seeing themselves and the world has been the only commodity on sale; the raw material of women's lives has not been processed and is not therefore available for use.

It is not just that men's values are put forward, it is also that women's are discarded. And the longer men stay in power, and retain the right to determine what society sees as important, the longer women are 'outside' and are seen to be displaying their 'unfitness for public office' . . . just as they did when they were outside education, and outside the political framework. When men decree what is significant and women disagree . . . then what women want is seen as insignificant and a sign that they are not to be taken seriously, not to be admitted to the circles of power. It is a nice interlocking – and supremely convenient – arrangement for men.

Fortunately, however, there are many women who won't accept this brand of 'logic' of the dominant group, and who refuse to believe that the values women hold are 'silly' no matter what men may say. Elizabeth Janeway (1980), Adrienne Rich (1979), Dorothy Smith (1978) and Dale Spender (1981a and b, 1982a and b) have followed Kate Millett and Mary Daly and are among the many who have insisted that the reason male experience is granted more significance and authority in our society has little to do with the *quality* of male experience but much to do with the dominant group's desire to value itself . . . and retain its power.

There have been numerous periods when women of the past have come together to forge their own meanings and understandings about male power, and the process has been revived over the last ten years as women have once more elaborated, refined and validated these insights in feminist networks and have extended their analysis of the establishment and maintenance of our male-dominated culture. One of the names that women have provided to describe the world from the position which women occupy is that of 'Gatekeeping'.

The 'gatekeepers' are the guardians of the culture. They are the ones who formulate the standards – and the justifications for those standards, the ones who pass judgment on what makes sense, what is credible. Gatekeepers are those, for example who can decree that the mind and body in our society are separate entities – regardless of the number of Indian mystics who suggest otherwise: they are the ones who can declare what constitutes a proper sexual relationship (in which nose-rubbing plays no part no matter how many members of the Eskimo or Maori community testify to its satisfactory nature, and in which the vaginal orgasm does play a part, no matter how many women express their in-comprehension). The guardians of the culture have very considerable powers – among them the power to declare as right and proper arrangements which suit them.

Generally, the theory of gatekeeping suggests that the people who hold decision-making positions in our society actually select the information and ideas that will be allowed to pass through the 'gates' and be incorporated into our culture. Specifically, the theory draws attention to the fact that our patriarchal society is purposefully arranged so that men fill the decision-making positions and become the keepers of the gates. On the basis of their experience and their understandings, men can allow entry to the informa-tion and ideas that they find appropriate and they can reject any material that they find unsuitable or unimportant. Gate-keeping thus provides men with a mechanism to promote their own needs and interests at the expense of all others. In doing so, it effectively ensures the continuation of a male-supremacist culture.

Undoubtedly, 'gatekeeping' is a term that arises out of women's experience of the world. Women are aware that we, as a group, are often kept from filling policy and decision-making positions and thus from acquiring the authority associated with them. 'Gatekeeping' provides us with a linguistic tool to name the techniques used to arrange our exclusion. We know that the social organization of our culture has evolved with male experience as the central reference point and that female experience has been excluded or eclipsed. We can see how men, already in positions of power, perceive other men as the best candidates for other positions of power, for within a male frame of reference, only male experience is valued. From this point we can under-stand how the authority granted to men becomes genuine authority because it is perpetually associated with men. Women do not have and cannot acquire authority in the same way. There is no need for men to set up committees and conspire personally to exclude women. The process of gate-keeping achieves the same effect in an impersonal way that allows men to dissociate themselves from any form of dis-crimination. At the same time, it works to reinforce the already pervasive myth of male superiority by continually making positions associated with power available to men.

If we consider the institutions that play major roles in determining our traditions and our way of life, women's exclusion from the upper levels is patently obvious. The exclusion may be structural and explicit as it is in the church, or it may be the result of social expectations that encourage consideration of certain roles as appropriate only for men. In either case it is an *arranged* exclusion and reserves decision-making roles for men. In government, the law, education, commerce, religion, medicine and the arts, women are still considered exceptional if they manage to acquire and hold on to positions of power and authority. Women at the upper levels are rarely seen as representatives of their sex but as female versions of the males who should rightfully hold the positions.

Whether or not men understand its workings or appreciate its significance, gatekeeping serves to reinforce male authority and to perpetuate male dominance. Because men have decreed that their logic, their reason and their truths are *human* logic, reason and truth, they have only to be honourable men in order to discriminate against women and then disclaim the practice. Their denial of women's truths, far from constituting a conspiracy, is transformed into the logical and reasonable application of high standards and high motives in the execution of their duty.

Naturally, many are puzzled by female accusations of gatekeeping and the connotations of active and political intervention. The protests ring loudly and clearly. Of course they would appoint women to positions of authority – if only there were any qualified; of course they would address women's issues – if only they were important; of course they would study women poets – if only there were some good enough. In their view, such decisions have nothing to do with 'gatekeeping'. They are based on *reason* and are the result of rational processes which uphold society's standards.

What is rarely considered though, especially by men, is that such standards are male standards. They are based on the tradition formed 'as the circle of those present builds on the work of the past' and in our society 'the circle of men whose writing and talk was significant to each other extends backwards in time as far as our records reach. What men were doing was relevant to men, was written by men about men for men' (Smith, 1978, p. 281). As the dominant group, men have been able to set their own standards and, through control of the organizational apparatus of society, to project and validate them as universal.

Out of these arrangements has emerged a social reality which automatically grants status and significance to men and their concerns. Available information from the past and the present provides justification for *all* of society to see men as the important group. Women, as members of a sub-dominant group, warrant less attention. Women's concerns are not regarded as major concerns and the information and ideas presented within society reflect this. In almost every situation where men and women both participate, men are given greater credibility and men's contributions are seen as having greater value. Because women are seen as less important than men, what women *say*, *do* and *think*, is considered less important than what men say, do and think. The end result is a whole way of life that reflects male dominance and continues to support it.

For example, when women talk, especially to each other, the assumption is that they 'gossip' and 'natter' and that what they say is of little consequence. Women themselves are frequently motivated to seek out 'male' conversation, not because they can participate in it – they are usually given few opportunities (Spender, 1980b) – but because they will be judged more favourably through their association with men than with other women. While men are regarded as the important members of society, acceptance by them, on any terms, can be construed as providing a form of status and prestige. The fact that many 'female' conversations deal with socially defined female experiences such as the preparation of food and the raising of children, and that these may constitute an essential area of communication for the survival of the species, is not usually given substantial value because women themselves are not valued. It is 'women's talk' and as such, regardless of its subject, it is seen as irrelevant to the real business of life that is embodied in men's talk. Men's verbal interactions are not termed 'gossip' or 'old husbands' tales' – even when they are discussing their sexual conquests or reminiscing about their youth. Apart from the notion that their talk is assumed to be important because they are important, men have been in control of language and of naming their own activities (Spender, 1980b) So while women 'chatter', 'natter', 'prattle' and 'nag', men 'discuss', 'debate' and 'analyse' with the inevitable outcome of reinforcing men's activities as significant and women's as unimportant, if not ridiculous. This is gatekeeping at its demonstrable best!

Regardless of the situation, interpretations and value judgments of women's and men's contributions consistently favour men. Even what women *do* is arranged to be less significant than what men do. The male-determined social structures that make men the obvious candidates to enter the public world of money, power and action also make women the obvious candidates to stay within the private world of family, home and personal relationships. What men do in the public world is called 'work' and consists of a range of occupations for which they are financially rewarded. These occupations are hierarchically structured and the higher the level reached, the more money, status and independence men can earn. But what women *do* in their private realm, performing nearly two-thirds of the world's work hours (UN Report, 1980), is regarded as 'non-work' (Oakley, 1974, p. 1). 'Non-work' involves no specific financial remuneration, no sickness or unemployment benefits, no pension and far from providing status and independence for women, forces them into direct dependence on a 'working' male. Production and reproduction in the home are not seen as comparable to the *real* business of production in which men are engaged. Certainly there is no correlation between women's increased productivity in the home and higher status or rates of pay. Indeed, as Ann Oakley explains it, the male concept of work as 'the expenditure of energy for financial gain, defines housework as the most inferior and marginal work of all' (Oakley, 1974, p. 4). As in the case of women talking, the effects are to diminish the status of women and to make it easier to discount our opinions. The reluctance of many women to write 'Occupation: *Housewife*' is understandable when we realize that to do so is to label ourselves, in society's terms, as inferior beings.

Thus are women's words and actions devalued because they differ visibly from the words and actions of men. But even invisible processes are subjected to negative assessment when women are involved. Regardless of their effectiveness in problem-solving or their contribution to a broader understanding of issues and events, women's *thoughts* are generally regarded by society as irrational, illogical and emotional. And of course, to the men who have named the world and who have appropriated logic, rationality and objectivity as the labels for their own (subjective) thinking patterns, women's thoughts – when they are different from men's – are automatically regarded as *ir*rational and *il*logical. Who but an irrational person would claim otherwise?

Whatever women say, do or think, society has been conditioned to view women as inferior to men. The whole assessment of women's roles and their position in society is part of what Molly Haskell refers to as 'the big lie'. Haskell claims that, 'The big lie perpetrated on Western Society is the idea of women's inferiority, a lie so deeply ingrained in our social behaviour that merely to recognize it is to risk unraveling the entire fabric of civilization' (quoted in Trahey, 1974, p. 61). It has been to prevent recognition of 'the big lie' that gatekeeping has evolved. Only by arranging for the exclusion of women from positions of power and from the registers of achievement can men ensure their own superiority and the privileges that accompany their superior status. It is not surprising that such great efforts have been expended in establishing a system of gatekeeping when it is understood that so much is at stake, for men.

From the time Aristotle stated in his seemingly 'logical' and dispassionate pronouncements that we should 'look upon the female state as being as it were a deformity, though one which occurs in the ordinary course of nature' (quoted in Rogers, 1968, p. 37), there has been within our culture, both a source and support for a tradition of the disparagement of women. And it has been well utilized! For spurious reasons, including our smaller brain size and our loss of sense during . menstruation, rationalizations for women's mental and physical inferiority have abounded. At the same time, evidence of male superiority – men's contributions to our culture, their 'better' understandings of the world and of women – have been deliberately promoted and presented as the truth.

The history that both women and men confront is men's history (Lewis, 1981). Our science is seen as a peculiarly male phenomenon (Arditti, 1980) and our sociology is the male study of males (Roberts, 1981a). Psychology is the application of male standards to human behaviour (Chesler, 1972; Miller, 1977) and health care as we know it, is the result of the deliberate appropriation of its practice by men during the nineteenth century (Ehrenreich and English, 1979). Religion, through careful editing and translating, presents us with a male deity (Spender, 1980b; Stanton, 1974) and our literary history has been shaped by the attitudes 'of white men towards non-whites and non-males' (Bernikow, 1974). In fact, all of the knowledge presented in our society as legitimate has arisen from a 'male as superior' perspective. Through the controls that gatekeeping has offered exclusively to men, male knowledge has been projected as universally true.

The overall result has been that women have been rendered invisible by the recorded data available in our culture, except in the roles that have been chosen for them by men and in relation to men. In accordance with Judaeo-Christian tradition, women are portrayed as conforming to the prototype of the Virgin Mary – essentially virtuous and submissive – as men's wives, mothers, muses and supporters – or they are presented in the mould of Eve as seductive temptresses – essentially evil – and the cause of the downfall of many a good man. No other roles for women are projected as valid. The tradition of female autonomy and women's centuries-old struggle against male oppression have been conveniently concealed. As Adrienne Rich says,

The entire history of women's struggle for self-determination has been muffled in silence over and over.

One serious cultural obstacle encountered by any
feminist writer is that each feminist work has tended to
be received as if it emerged from nowhere; as if each of us
had lived, thought, and worked without any historical
past or contextual present. This is one of the ways in
which women's work and thinking has been made to
seem sporadic, errant, orphaned of any tradition of its
own. (Rich, 1979, p. 11)

In an extensive study of women's acknowledged and
unacknowledged contributions to our culture, Dale Spender
in *Women of Ideas* (1982a) has revealed the tremendous
amount of women's knowledge that has been generated
during the last few centuries and the tremendous efforts
made by the establishment to minimize and discredit that
knowledge. Spender's research proves unequivocally that
gatekeeping has played a major role in preserving the
inequality of the sexes in all aspects of life and to all men's
advantage.

Thus the questions that we are now invited to ask about
our cultural heritage are quite different from those we have
asked in the past. Rather than trying to discover why there
are no 'great' women artists (Nochlin, 1977), we want to know
who made up the notion of greatness and on what criteria it
was established. Instead of asking why the long association
between women and writing has produced so few 'great'
women writers, we want to know why it was important to
rank women's written words and to discriminate between the
words of women and men. Whose interests, after all, have
been served by differentiation on the basis of sex and by
continually judging male contributions as 'greater' than
women's? With this question in mind, we want to ask what
may be an even more pertinent question, namely why *any*
women writers, thinkers, scientists or artists have been
included at all in the recording of our culture!

In other words the area of inquiry has shifted from
assessing the creative work of women to recognizing the
destructive work that men have done by acting as gatekeepers. Immediately we see the need to explore the techniques men have used to limit women's access to the public

world and to eclipse women's contributions from our culture. Immediately we see the connections between the assessment and recording of achievement, and the processes and people involved in publishing.

For centuries the institution of publishing has been instrumental in determining *what will be made publicly known* and publishing has been the gate through which material has been obliged to pass in order to qualify for inclusion in our written records. Publishers have acted as guardians of the gate and private, written words have required their approval in order to be transformed into public, printed words. With the focus now on publishers as guardians, we realize that approval for women's actions and women's written words has not often been forthcoming -- especially when those words and actions have challenged men's interests in a significant way.

Like other media industries, publishing has been and is still very much a 'man's world' (Strainchamps, 1974). 'Women are concentrated in the lowest ranks . . . and [there are] virtually none at the top' (West, 1978, p. 6). Decisions in publishing are made by men and the processes involved in publishing are controlled by men. In the selection of people to fill policy-making positions and in the selection of material to be made publicly available, male consciousness is the reference point. Men make the best candidates in the system that men have devised and thus become the gatekeepers.

But knowledge about gatekeeping techniques provides us with an opportunity to deconstruct the controls that men have been using within publishing. Research into *their* activities rather than our own cannot fail to expose their manipulation of public, printed words in order to promote their own view of the world and their associated positions of dominance. The bias and self-interest that have given us a published heritage of men's truths and an *unpublished heritage* of excluded and discarded women's truths now become glaringly obvious. It is becoming increasingly difficult to deny that the *unpublished heritage* exists, not because women's perceptions are less valid or truthful than men's, but because it has suited those in power to remove from public awareness any material that could threaten or challenge their authority and privileges. With the political nature of men's actions so named, the purposeful nature of our value system and social structures becomes quite clear. Within publishing, as elsewhere, men stand accused of subterfuge and gross intervention in the recording of our heritage and the creation of our social reality. It is an accusation for which there can be no 'rational' defence!

Chapter 2

The Printed Word

Our society has long been a literate one. Whilst other societies kept alive their customs, ideology and knowledge through oral traditions, through dance, corroboree and ritual, we abandoned these methods and adopted *the printed word* as the means of storing our heritage and transmitting our culture. Now, as a result of dealing for many years with the printed word as the medium of organization and education, we have invested print with the status of recorder of our civilization and conveyor of our cultural truths.

Because print has traditionally been associated with scholarship and learning and has at various times in our history been seen to provide the catalyst for social change, the avenue to personal salvation and the source of insight and knowledge (Zimet, 1977, p. 13), we have built a tradition of reverence and respect for words in print. There has been a subtle inculcation of the idea that print is associated with legitimacy and we have been led to believe that printed words warrant special consideration. Ideas and information, especially when they have been issued by the 'authorities' or have remained in print over long periods, tend to be accepted as embodying 'truths' that we should heed. Consequently, we have not only come to regard print as the legitimate recorder and transmitter of truth and knowledge, we have unconsciously come to accept print as their creator.

There is nothing intrinsically wrong with print acquiring prestige or status as a form of communication. In fact, the printed word has offered a very efficient means of recording and communicating information and ideas – at least for those who could read and write. What is disturbing about the role print has acquired is the evidence of manipulation that has been involved in its production and dissemination. Beyond simple efficiency, there have been many other factors associated with its adoption as the authoritative form of communication and the theory of gatekeeping makes these factors quite explicit.

Until relatively recently very few people have had access to the literacy skills required for first-hand knowledge of the printed word and there is considerable evidence that this has been a deliberate rather than an accidental development. Women, children and the 'lower classes' were kept ignorant of printed truths except as they were explained by educated men or promoted through the systems of organization that educated men controlled (and this is still the case in many societies: again UN statistics (1980) reveal that each year the gap grows between women's illiteracy rates and those of men). The level of resistance mounted by these same educated men to women who also wished to gain access to an education testifies to the sort of deliberate gatekeeping practices that enabled those in control of the printed word to maintain their control. (See Rita McWilliams-Tullberg, 1977, for an account of 'Women and degrees at Cambridge University, 1862-1897', and Albie Sachs and Joan Hoff Wilson, 1978, on *Sexism and the Law*.) It was not until a changing society gave rise to a need for more, literate people that the idea of mass education became popular. By that time, controls over what would be published in print were well established in the hands of a previously educated male elite.

Obviously it makes a great deal of sense to the group who act as the decision-makers in any society (particularly when they represent a numerical minority) to have gatekeeping privileges over at least one form of communication. The ability to determine what will appear within that form, whether it is print, television, radio or any other, allows considerable influence on the social reality. Even with universal literacy, it becomes possible to control the content and the form of messages sent from the organizers to the organized.

If it is also possible to establish the chosen medium of communication as an ostensibly neutral one, the medium itself can serve as an agent of social control. By convincing people that it is impartial and objective, its message is interpreted as the result of neutral decision-making and there need be little awareness of a connection between the interests of the decision-makers and the general quality and way of life of the society. It can be an effective method of creating 'willing' rather than 'forced' slaves. (See discussion of J. S. Mill in Alice S. Rossi, 1974.)

When the printed word is considered in this light, gate-keeping patterns become visible. It seems just a little too convenient in our society, where one group is dominant, that the form of communication chosen to carry the greatest prestige and authority is also the form that offers the dominant group most opportunities for intervention and control during its production.

Whether the specific genre being dealt with is fact or fiction (and there is an argument put forward by women that it is often difficult to differentiate between men's 'facts' and women's 'fiction', and vice versa), at any of four or more stages in the selection, production and distribution of the printed word, there are opportunities for active intervention by those who arrange its transformation from a written manuscript into an article available for purchase. From the time the initial editorial decision is made about what topics will be seen as significant, there are numerous occasions when the original words and ideas of any manuscript can be altered. Editors select the material they deem most appropriate; 'experts' referee the manuscripts and can accept, reject or recommend changes to them; editors can guide, influence or coerce writers into modifying or expanding their material and some member of the publishing group decides how many copies will actually be printed. Ultimately, decision-makers involved at various stages in the processes of publishing can shape the final product to suit their own needs and interests.

Even after the words have appeared in print, the status they will eventually acquire can be influenced through gate-keeping controls. Once they are bound, they are treated like any other commodity to be marketed and distributed. If they qualify as 'brand-name' merchandise (written by a well-known author or published through a prestigious publishing house), their chances for substantial sales figures (the mark of success) are higher than those of the 'no-name' products which require a different sort of promotion and push to receive similar ratings. If the contacts exist to have them reviewed by important sources such as *Publishers' Weekly* or *The New York Times* in America or by *The Times* in England (examples of the power we have invested in the printed word to determine our 'truths'), and if resources are available for extensive promotion, display and distribution, then they have the potential to be commercially successful.

With academic publications, where commercial success is not necessarily the criteria for recognition of material as significant, the peculiar situation exists where there may even be little connection between what is promoted as impressive material and what is meaningful to its audience. Dr Scott Armstrong has demonstrated with his 'Dr Fox phenomenon' that the assessment of material in the field of business management (and there is no evidence to assume that the same principles do not apply in other forms of academic literature) is so irrational and artificial that the more unintelligible a piece of prose appears, the more likely it is to be rated as impressive and scholarly. Armstrong suggests that those 'researchers who want to impress their colleagues should write less intelligible papers' and that 'journals seeking respectability should publish less intelligible papers' (quoted in Leapman, 1980).

Whether the material is 'academic' or 'popular', the assigning of significance to printed words has less to do with universal concepts of merit than with personal opinion and biases. Until recently, books that did not appear in hardcover form were unlikely to be reviewed in any of the important forums because they were not acknowledged by reviewers as worthy of serious attention (Harms, 1979; Callil, 1981). Apparently the criteria of importance applied to printed words are based on their texture and their unintelligibility. What this has meant for the presentation of ideas that have not *felt* good or that have been *clearly articulated* needs little elaboration. They have probably passed without notice into the literary archives or been shredded and recycled for the production of less intelligible and better-feeling messages.

Other arrangements exist to rank some printed words as more significant than others. Where the gatekeepers in publishing leave off as the guardians of truth, knowledge and social mores, agencies like schools, colleges, universities, libraries and book clubs take over. Their selection of material for texts, reference books, authors to be studied and titles to be promoted, plays a substantial part in establishing the notion that some printed words are more legitimate than others and consequently that some messages are more valid than others. A concept of excellence that relates to the personal and political choices of publishers and social agencies rather than to a consensus among readers, comes into being. Whatever is chosen and named as the 'best' material available is recorded as representative of our choices even though our own experiences play no part in the judgment. In literature, as Tillie Olsen has pointed out,

Achievement: as gauged by what supposedly designates it: appearance in twentieth-century literature courses, required reading lists, textbooks, quality anthologies, the year's best, the decade's best, the fifty year's best, consideration by critics or in current reviews – *one woman writer for every twelve men* (8 percent women, 92 percent men). (Olsen, 1979, p. 24)

These figures, while not necessarily evidence of sheer misogyny, are indicative of the gatekeeping arrangements that put men's words into print and have men's thoughts regarded as universally representative. The values and ideas that are embodied in the eleven out of the twelve works rated as the 'best' are products of a male-as-dominant perspective and perpetuate the tradition of male supremacy. Alternative realities, as defined by the other half of the population, do not appear as often in the 'best' work and cannot acquire the same legitimacy. The printed word, as most of us receive it, encodes a political bias that promotes men's right to name the world and to validate *their* names as *our* cultural truths.

From a feminist perspective, it is clear that the status and content of the printed word have been shaped and determined by men through the same techniques that have allowed our value system and social structures to develop as products of male experience and male consciousness. From the time when only a few privileged men were familiar with print until today when a few privileged men control its selection and production, women have not usually been permitted to participate in its making and are minimally represented in the truths that print has created and communicated to society. With print occupying a revered and influential position in our culture, this means that the very medium used to set the parameters of our knowledge is 'man'-made and 'man'-controlled. The *we* who have used the printed word for so long to name *our* world and to define *our* roles within it, refers almost exclusively to men. Print, the conveyor of truth and creator of knowledge, does not reflect human experience and universal truth. It stands as a mirror for men and reflects the values of a male-supremacist society. From any perspective, concern over the role that the printed word has come to play in our society is amply justified.

Such concern makes us realize that it is not accidental that the primary sources of our knowledge and understanding of the world exist in printed form. Our laws, references, texts, journals and literary classics appear in print because it is the medium that offers most opportunities for control. Nor is it accidental that none of these forms is visibly tarnished by the brush of commercialism. In spite of the very commercial nature of the processes involved in their creation (West, 1978), our most authoritative books and journals do not carry advertisements or any blatantly commercial trappings. When their *back* pages do make reference to other books in a series or recommend other titles, they are presented like academic reading lists and certainly not as crass advertisements which might detract from the ostensibly impartial and objective knowledge contained within their covers. Their integrity is not to be doubted.

Other forms of communication, less amenable to total

and considered control, are visibly associated with commercial interests and their truths are less persuasive. Television, a new and undoubtedly a major influence on the behaviour and expectations of its regular viewers, does not compete on the same level as the printed word in terms of authority or prestige. The 'truths' promoted by television, especially in North America where television's primary function is entertainment, are of dubious authority, at least on some occasions. Understanding that programmes compete for commercial ratings also means understanding that a certain amount of manipulation is involved in their selection and presentation. The advertisements that punctuate programmes with monotonous regularity and which employ every conceivable technique of persuasion on potential consumers, inevitably detract from the impartiality of the messages that television conveys. It is perhaps not too cynical to suggest this as the reason for some North American programmes actually acknowledging feminism as a positive and growing movement. There need be little fear that viewers will take it too seriously.

Certainly British feminists have shown that the image of feminism, promoted with the non-commercial air of authority and objectivity through the BBC, is far from positive. Elaine Morgan notes that the top decision-makers are mainly men and 'they would have to be superhuman if their decisions were to be totally unaffected by their own instincts as to what is exciting and what is boring' (Morgan, 1979, p. 212). I doubt that their decisions are instinctive rather than reasoned and a recent breakdown of scripted material for adult viewing reveals that they are certainly not superhuman. 'Women contribute to the BBC something around ten percent' (Morgan, 1979, p. 211). Helen Baehr notes that BBC programmes that have dealt with feminism have usually managed to present it as some form of distasteful aberration and that feminists (women's libbers) are likely to be represented as 'unnatural, ridiculous and wrong' (Baehr, 1980, p.38).

Journalism, film and radio broadcasting all present more difficulties than the printed word in terms of control of their message and all have developed with commercial aspects that diminish their authority. Reservation by the public about their 'truths' is not unusual. The evidence of hierarchies within journalism – whereby one newspaper or magazine is considered better than others because it adopts a particular style even though all eventually carry the same 'news' – encourages a certain amount of scepticism amongst consumers. The investigative and competitive nature of journalism and the errors frequently made (and sometimes acknowledged) impinge on our consciousness in a way we do not normally associate with the material presented in texts and references. Film, with its connotations of Hollywood, movie-stars and stuntmen leaves us partially aware of its fairy-tale quality even when its 'truths' come close to our own experience. Radio broadcasting, possibly because we cannot see what is taking place, carries with it a notion of artificiality – of technical rather than human communication – even when its message is direct and spontaneous. Ironically, the medium of print, whose message is probably most susceptible to intervention and control, is the form of communication that we accept as most impartial and objective.

Whether it is fact or fiction and although we know that at several stages people have been involved in selecting and editing its content and form, we are generally satisfied to accept that print, when it appears in its most authoritative forms, is true. We rarely challenge the expertise or the motives of those doing the selecting; we rarely question the validity of the content in terms of our own experience. We assume that if it does not match with our experience, then we are probably wrong. We do not confront the possibility that print may represent only one of the many available 'truths' on a particular subject and that others may be being kept from us. And why should we? We have not been encouraged to challenge the legitimacy of the printed word. We have been urged to accept it. The idea that there may be a political dimension involved in its selection does not therefore usually occur to us and the connections between our published heritage and a particular group of men who have traditionally controlled it are not made. The notion of an *unpublished heritage* of discarded and excluded work, that might have provided us with a quite different reality from the one which we are so often prepared to accept as inevitable, rarely surfaces as a topic for discussion.

For where else do legitimate topics come from other than the dialogue and consensus between the people with the authority and power to name them? And why would they publicize and draw attention to topics that might create unnecessary problems?

Thomas Kuhn (1970) points out that those who are the experts in a particular field tend to guard the validity of their knowledge and suppress 'novelties' which challenge or reflect unfavourably on its authority. There is no reason to think that the experts in publishing or the people they consult during decision-making are any different. This holds immense implications for the material selected for publication. It means that it is quite possible that publishers have rejected material when it has challenged their views and it is very possible that writers, especially those in the academic community where the pressure to publish is strong, may have tailored their material to fit the prevailing orthodoxy (Spender, 1981a). According to June Arnold, this is precisely what women have had to do in their dealings with commercial presses – 'to pre-program your mind to work from male values . . . or you may as well save your pencil for the grocery list' (Arnold, 1976, p. 18). Even if the writer recognizes the 'truths' of her work as *untrue* when they are programmed to fit the male mould, they may still become accepted as a valid part of our cultural heritage.

Along similar lines, Gene Maeroff contends that many writers (especially younger members of academe and women) suspect that they are at a disadvantage in competing with more established researchers for the scarce space available for publication in academic journals. Increasingly they are calling for a system of 'blind refereeing' which, by maintaining their anonymity, might prevent referees from being influenced by reputations – the writer's or that of the institution with which they are associated (Maeroff, 1979). This may go part of the way toward removing the subjective element involved in the selection of material for print. But it does not, from a feminist viewpoint, eliminate the 'male-as-norm' elements while referees, reviewers and 'experts' are predominantly male and form part of a network of similar-minded people. What is traditional, conventional and within their frame of reference and therefore supports the existing scheme of values will still be more appealing than that which is new, unorthodox or threatening to the *status quo*.

What we are left with is a printed heritage that gives legitimacy and authority to a male-defined social reality. In order to change that reality to one that is representative of human experience, it is essential to expose the political dimension of the gatekeeping arrangements that operate in the production and presentation of the printed word. We are led again to a consideration of the processes and the people involved in the instititution of publishing.

Chapter 3

The Publishing Mystique

The extraordinary status granted to the printed word as a form of communication is matched by the equally extraordinary privileges enjoyed by its producers in the publishing industry. From any perspective, they are allowed unusual freedom to determine their own principles and practices and are given unusual absolution from accountability for them.

Of all businesses that operate in a middle-man capacity between supply and demand factors there is probably no other that offers the sort of control that is available to publishers. The supply with which they deal – the thoughts, ideas and research of other people – can be accepted, rejected, reshaped and in most cases commissioned according to the personal judgment of the publisher or consensus amongst his colleagues. Their expertise and their standards, although unnamed and unspecified, provide the criteria on which all raw material will be assessed.

On the demand side, it is possible for publishers to either withhold or publicize information about what material is available and through huge promotional campaigns to actually create a demand for their chosen products. Conglomerate organizations such as Doubleday, Macmillan, McGraw-Hill and others with enormous financial and technical resources control numerous presses and distribution outlets and allow the commercial publishing fraternity to dictate the terms on which their products will be sold – where, how many and for how much. At the same time they are able to influence the buying patterns of those who have money available to spend on their publications.

The situation currently exists where commercial publishers have gained so much control over the production and dissemination of the printed word that neither the writers who supply the original ideas and images nor the readers who eventually demand them have any guarantee that their needs will be acknowledged or met. Decision-making is entirely in the hands of the publishers; the values they promote and the standards they set are their business and their business alone!

Other institutions that form part of the organizational apparatus of our society and which are involved in the production and maintenance of the prevailing system of values are usually subjected, formally or informally, to some form of public scrutiny.

Governments, for example, responsible for legislating many aspects of our lives, are periodically obliged to present themselves for public assessment. Our 'free' press is vigilant in providing details about government representatives if it is thought they might inform public opinion about platforms, policies or personalities – or, of course, sell more papers. It is a fundamental principle of democracy that politicians, whether elected or appointed, are responsible and accountable to the people they represent. The exposure through the press of the now infamous Watergate scandal in America which implicated top-level officials in corruption and amoral practices is not really surprising in a society which prides itself on its allegedly 'free' press and on its system of responsible government.

Within the institution of education, avenues exist for formal training of its practitioners and for the study of its principles and practices. Professional training involves courses comprised of accumulated (albeit selected) information about educational theory and practice. Entire undergraduate and postgraduate departments exist solely for the purpose of studying education and while little credibility may be given by educational policy-makers to data that does not appeal to them, a forum does exist for dialogue to take place, and resources are made available for research and study in the field.

Even the business world is regarded as an area where it is considered important for information about managers and management decisions to be made publicly available. We who are affected by management decisions see it as reasonable to have access to relevant information. We expect that people who have power in several areas such as commerce *and* government declare their interests so they cannot take advantage of 'inside' information. Corruption and mismanagement by those in power is considered scoop material by media forms that see reporting on the business world as an integral part of their role. Lobby groups and unions have developed to protect the interests of employers and employees. Existing and codified ways of naming and dealing with problems are well established.

But publishing as an institution is subjected to no such criticism or exposure. There is no concept that publishers should be accountable for their decisions about what will appear in printed form even though there is a substantial argument that they as effectively legislate the parameters of our ideological existence as do governments and other agencies. There is no notion that the public should be informed of the goals or motives of the individuals and companies who control the selection and dissemination of the printed word, nor even that we need to know who they are.

It might conceivably be assumed that the institution of publishing has deliberately devised a system to repel any public involvement or familiarity with its procedures. There are few, if any, courses outside the publishing networks which are directly addressed to publishing as an activity and which might prompt a critique of the industry. There is no section in daily papers devoted to discussion or dialogue relating to the criteria used in the selection of manuscripts for publication; it is not a 'topic' offered in courses at schools or other educational establishments. In spite of its exceptional character as a powerful agent of propaganda, any information that does exist about publishing tends to be directed towards its operation as a business and rarely to its potential for manipulation or its social responsibilities. It would seem that publishers and publishing are regarded as sufficiently removed from the centres of economic and political power to be unaffected by corruption or manipulation. They alone are given freedom to operate on the basis of 'pure artistic integrity'.

The potential for gatekeeping under these circumstances is excessive, to say the least. Far removed from public accountability, publishers are free to invoke 'standards' (which after all are merely a consensus between a group of people as to what is appropriate, correct or marketable) and behind them to transform personal value judgments into ostensibly neutral and justifiable decisions. The 'standards' serve to substantiate claims that their decisions are based on some 'objective' and higher authority to which the uninitiated can have no access and no redress. The projected image and the one that seems to be generally accepted by the public is that publishers are the 'experts'; that their decisions and their choices are impartial and that the work that they present in print has been chosen on a fair and rational basis.

That the public has accepted this image without demur is not really surprising. Publishers are in a position to censor what will and what will not be published about the industry, and it is understandable that the connections between what we are presented with as knowledge and truth and publishers' personal and commercial interests have not been widely promoted. I know of no prestigious publisher who has agreed to print and actively promote an exposé of the publishing industry and have no doubt that this book will not match current bestsellers in terms of financial rewards or promotional budget.

Information that attests to the 'professional' and often humorous eccentricities of the publishing fraternity is not so difficult to find. Much of it serves to protect the image of publishers as exceptional beings and to create a mystique around the processes involved in publishing. In the Introduction to the Seventh Edition of *The Truth About Publishing* (1960), Sir Stanley Unwin reveals that the following 'curious and unusual combination of qualifications' is desirable in a publisher: 'Something much more than knowledge is needed, namely judgment and what for want of a better word I can only call 'flair', in the selection of manuscripts to be published and the number of copies it is expedient to print' (Unwin, 1960).

What a very convenient rationale! The association of the publisher's judgment with the intangible quality of 'flair' immediately invests publishers with qualities to which most ordinary mortals dare not aspire. Without this 'power of scent, instinctive discernment' (*Shorter Oxford English Dictionary*), we cannot presume to question the decisions of publishers nor even establish the criteria on which they make their selections. The process is apparently magical.

It does however seem possible to an outsider that such 'flair' may be a quality similar to 'female intuition', which far from being a mysterious gift seems likely to be a combination of skills, 'developed through long practice in reading small signals . . .' (Miller, 1977, p. 10). It is very probable that people who work within a fairly closed industry and who operate within networks specifically established to provide them with relevant and current information about available writers and marketable topics, will develop the contacts, skills and experience that will enable them to make informed decisions. But to promote these skills as unique qualities is to create a mystique about publishers as special people with special talents whose expertise is not to be challenged. That the mystique works extremely well to keep out ideas, images, and people which might undermine an otherwise comfortable existence needs to be considered. So too does the popular notion of publishers as an elite group of qualified men, totally removed from prejudice, bias or personal interests, poring over manuscripts and dedicated to the discovery of new talent and literary merit. Evidence both past and current indicates that this is just not so!

The past ten years have produced several publications dealing with the publishing industry. It is not inconsistent with ideas presented earlier in this book to claim that those which offer some sort of critique or exposé of the industry have been put out by small alternative presses, and that the commercial presses have concentrated more on updating and reviewing the plethora of 'how-to' books which allegedly provide all the information required to 'crack' the publishing code and 'break into print'. (It may be significant that 'how-to' books are presently enjoying a high marketability rating.) Generally, such guides offer names, addresses and requirements that must be fulfilled if unsolicited manuscripts are to be considered by established publishing companies. But there seems to be a credibility gap between what publishers state as required and what they actually accept. One large publishing company for example, listed in several of the handbooks and stating explicitly how submissions should be made, is also noted (elsewhere) for receiving 10,000 unsolicited manuscripts each year and for rejecting them all!

From the information provided by publishers about what they do accept in the way of unsolicited manuscripts (see Chapter 6) it is clear that the numbers are very limited. I do not think it cynical to propose that the handbooks which are presented to the public do not facilitate publication but instead serve to make it more difficult. By projecting the myth that there is some rational and knowable 'standard' that writers must attain before their work is acceptable, writers are kept busily writing and re-writing in order to 'crack the code' and reach the standard, while publishers, removed from pressure or accountability, can pursue their real work of commissioning and editing manuscripts that suit their personal or company requirements. In spite of the variety and availability of the 'how-to-books', it may be that the most honest and reliable piece of information about publishing has come from *Time* magazine which stated, 'it is virtually impossible for an unknown author to break into print' (in Henderson, 1980, Preface). This statement is public acknowledgment (which few openly dispute) that new ideas and new knowledge from people not associated with an institution or established network are not likely to receive exposure or distribution. Its implications for feminism and women's concern with change are clear, in that we should not expect any help from the commercial publishing industry. Their stated concerns centre around making money from backing those ideas and people who are already familiar and marketable, and their unstated concerns are with supporting rather than subverting the system which has allowed them to progress into positions of privilege and power. We would be unrealistic to expect that commercial publishers might willingly involve themselves in a movement to bring about social change.

Few of the other publications about publishing that are readily available have attempted a systematic analysis of the industry and how it works. *The Publish-It-Yourself Handbook* (Henderson, 1980) offers a good example of the familiar expression that 'commercial publishers don't publish anything that hasn't been published before' and is a collection of statements and comments on how to avoid the traditional publishing processes. The editor, Bill Henderson, makes his attitude towards commercial publishers quite explicit in his comment, 'They [writers] know that commercial houses can't always be relied upon to recognize talent' (Henderson, 1980, Preface). Implicit in this statement and in the example quoted of Jerzy Kosinski's book, *Steps*, is the idea that there is no objective and rational standard which publishers use in the selection of manuscripts. Kosinski's book, the winner of the 1969 National Book Award in the United States, was resubmitted to agents and publishers as an unsolicited manuscript and was rejected by them *all*, including the original 'discoverer' of the book.

Examples like this of the irrationality of publishing decisions lead one to wonder how publishers defend their notions of merit and 'standards'. Perhaps this sort of inconsistency in part explains why the publishing industry has developed its protective mystique. It would certainly be difficult for the publishers involved in the reassessment of Kosinski's book to reconcile their projected image of rationality and expertise with the inconsistency that they demonstrated. It is far easier for them to dismiss such examples as minor transgressions from their usual noble path than to admit that most decisions are based on the same subjective values and processes. There is no rational explanation for such irrational decision-making. There is no way for courses dealing with the principles and practices of publishing to be offered to the public without precipitating the collapse of the whole commercial publishing industry.

Also in *The Publish-It-Yourself Handbook*, Henderson

alludes to the myth (a myth which most commercial publishers would no doubt be pleased to foster), that written work is somehow inferior if not accepted by a commercial press. He goes on to give many examples of do-it-yourself successes and dispels the notion, intellectually if not emotionally, that huge capital resources are required for self-publishing. But in advocating self-publishing, Henderson is battling against overwhelming odds. One book or even several books cannot break down the influence and control wielded by big commercial presses in the publishing world. The existence of more, alternative methods of publishing, operating in a marginal capacity, while commercial publishers retain their hold over supply and demand factors, will not bring about major changes in the system. Not until the patriarchal and commercial assumptions that now underlie the practices of publishers are replaced with genuinely universal values will the material selected for publication change dramatically in its composition. Ironically, it may not be until print no longer forms the primary method for the communication of ideas that the printed word will come to reflect the concerns of all members of society.

Anaïs Nin, whose books *Winter of Artifice* and *Under a Glass Bell* were initially rejected by American publishers because they were 'uncommercial' (although they had already been published in France and had received positive reviews), also recommends the self-publishing technique. Of commercial publishers she notes the desire for 'quick and large returns' and claims that they back their choices with 'advertising disguised as literary judgement' (Nin, 1980, p. 31). Her experiences indicate that commercial publishers are not primarily concerned with pursuing or creating a literary heritage that represents the thoughts of each generation of thinkers and writers. They are more likely to choose and promote work and writers whose marketability is established and whose ideas are traditional and familiar. What this implies for those members of society whose perceptions have been considered outside the 'mainstream' of literary concerns and outside the particular perspective engendered by white, middle-class male experience, is significant. Their opportunities for establishing a published heritage that

grants validity to their experience and their point of view is
almost non-existent.

The commercial aspect of publishing that Anaïs Nin
decries has also been criticized by Celeste West and Valerie
Wheat in *The Passionate Perils of Publishing* (1978).
Published by a small, independent press, the book does
provide informed criticism of the commercial publishing
industry, 'whose overriding concern is cash, not communication' (West and Wheat, 1978, p. 3). West points to the trend
amongst commercial publishers to merge into huge conglomerate organizations which control all aspects of publishing –
acquisitions, marketing, distribution – and to effectively
exclude smaller, independent companies from competing in
terms of price or availability. West also draws attention to
some of the implications of publishing being a commercial
rather than a cultural activity, and to sexism within the
industry which she claims is controlled by 'rich, white,
heterosexual men' (ibid., p. 6). Not only is material for
publication selected on the basis of its commercial potential
rather than its cultural significance, it is also chosen by a
particular group of men who are at liberty to make personal
choices and promote them as impartial and legitimate.

The appearance in 1978 of *How To Get Happily Published – A Complete and Candid Guide* by Judith Applebaum
and Nancy Evans, themselves involved in the publishing
world as editors and writers, signalled an attempt to de-
mystify the publishing industry. But the fact that it was
published by Harper & Row should have registered that it
would be far from a radical exposé of the industry. Certainly
the book achieves its stated goal of providing 'guidance to get
through the publishing thicket' (p. xiv) but it never seriously
questions why such a 'thicket' exists or whose interests it
serves.

Without an appreciation (which they may well have had
but were unable to present) of the political aspect involved in
the industry's promotion of inconsistencies in order to maintain its non-accessibility and non-accountability, the authors
are obliged to present seemingly contradictory evidence. On
one hand they agree that the industry is made up of 'flesh and
blood men and women, who invevitably alter the rules to fit

personal and practical demands' (p. 2), and on the other they claim that publishing is a 'rational and manageable activity' (p. 1).

Consequently, editors' 'mistakes' (p. 5) are viewed as just another hurdle to be overcome and although they state that a rejected manuscript 'may well reflect more unfavourably on the editors ability than yours' (p. 5), the implication exists that it is the writer who must negotiate the publishing 'labyrinth' and not the publishers who should state their interests and motives and declare their personal and non-rational bias.

So, at the moment, the mystique of publishing remains intact, as does the male-dominated society out of which it has grown and which it supports. The idea that written material must meet certain requirements in order to be marketable is often merely a facade allowing publishers to select material that suits their own personal and political purposes. If the marketability rationale had any credibility and publishers really were the experts that we have been led to believe they are, then all books would be bestsellers. Round-table conferences where acquisitions editors presented their recommendations, where referees' reports were given, where marketing experts divulged the latest trends, would preclude the possibility of errors and all chosen manuscripts would prove popular and significant.

But potential marketability and publishers' 'flair' are not the only factors involved in selection decisions. The personal values and perspectives of the decision-makers are also involved and because the decision-makers are predominantly men an inevitable political factor is also introduced. If perchance the marketability rationale were suddenly removed from publishing and publishers were encouraged to select material simply on the basis of what they considered 'excellent', it is not likely that their selections would alter very much. 'Excellence' in literature is a culturally loaded concept and what seems excellent to the privileged few in publishing may be quite different from the notions of excellence held by people in less privileged situations. Yet the publishing mystique allows the perspective of the few to prevail and male dominance continues to be fostered as the norm. As far as feminists are concerned, the removal of commercial considerations from the publishing agenda might even curtail the publication of feminist material. Without the possibility of the lucrative market that feminist material currently represents, publishers may feel no need at all to put feminist thoughts or ideas into print. They may even feel perfectly justified in protecting society from such a departure from 'excellence'.

The freedom and privileges granted to publishers both as business people and as culture-makers really do warrant further investigation. The many opportunities that publishers are afforded to control ideas and knowledge (thereby determining much of our social reality) should be a publicly addressed issue; the interests and the specifically male orientation of commercial publishers should be declared as openly as feminist publishers have always declared their feminist politics. Only then will the balance of power, now tilted in men's favour in publishing and in society generally, begin to shift towards an equilibrium.

Chapter 4

A Heritage of Harassment

Beyond the recognition of a general pattern of social control of women by men, contemporary feminist insights have revealed some of the specific techniques that have been used to oppress women. Understanding that it has been very important for men to exclude women from positions of power where they might establish an ongoing tradition and eventually challenge male authority, feminists have identified one of these techniques as the *sexual harassment* of women. The term refers to women's experience of men's attitudes and behaviour, particularly in the shared workplace. It names situations where men expose women to difficulties 'ranging from subtle psychological coercion to gross physical abuse' (Backhouse and Cohen, 1978, p. 1). Lin Farley in her analysis of this sort of harassment claims,

> Work is the key element in understanding sexual harassment, because this is the prize men are controlling through their extortion. . . . The consequences of such extortion – being denied work or being forced out of work or being intimidated on the job as a result of male sexual aggression – are at the heart of the problem of sexual harassment. (Farley, 1978, p.11)

It seems that sexual harassment of women workers has increased not only as more women have entered the workforce generally, but especially where they have entered areas previously reserved for men. In the latter case, many men have reacted to women's presence by treating women in their traditional role as men's property rather than as co-workers who happen to be women. Such men apparently feel quite justified in exhibiting behaviour ranging from 'sexist' remarks, through bottom-pinching, to the many reported incidents of males in superior positions demanding sexual favours of their subordinates. However, in part owing to the influence of the current women's movement and in part owing to women's rightful indignation at being treated differently from their fellow workers simply because they are members of the other sex, women are becoming increasingly aware of the implications of their treatment in the work-place. The many articles and books that have become available on the subject since it was actually *named* as an issue indicate that many women now recognize it as harassment that is specifically sexual in nature.

Further, many women are coming to understand that the problem is not one that can be solved by women. As in so many other areas – such as rape – where men have insisted through the laws and social customs they have established that women are responsible for men's vicious and irresponsible behaviour – it really does not make any difference how women behave. Even if women modify their appearance or their general demeanour, it is the fact that they are women that makes men feel free to treat them with less humanity. The problem can only be rectified through a change in *men's* attitudes and behaviour.

To contemporary women, sexual harassment can clearly be seen as a phenomenon arising from a society which condones male dominance and female subordination – a society which encourages men to consider women as objects who exist primarily in relation to men. In societies which operate on this premise, as do most Western societies, it has been men's prerogative to establish the norm for female/male relationships, with the result that our history is one in which men have granted themselves the right to beat wives who did not obey them; they saw fit to deprive wives of all property and all rights to children; they encoded the idea that adultery for women was a far more serious offence than for men. In the workplace they established that women should receive less money for the work they did; they denied women access to the more lucrative and prestigious forms of employment; they felt justified in exposing women to psychological and physical abuse. In both situations they arranged that female/male relationships would depend upon whether or not men *chose* to use the power available to them to exploit and harass women. Needless to say, many have done so in the past and continue to do so today.

Sexual harassment, when viewed as an aspect of *men's* behaviour (rather than as the result of *women's* behaviour), provides a new dimension to the study of women in society and especially to those women from the past who first ventured into traditionally male areas. As more of our history as a people is reassessed from a feminist perspective, it is possible to see that sexual harassment is not a phenomenon that has arisen recently but one which has been practised on women *whenever* they have assumed positions to challenge male dominance and authority. In most cases and in most areas women who have 'usurped' male territory have been met with harassment of one form or another because of their sex. In the world of letters particularly, women have suffered considerably for their intrusions and our published and our unpublished heritage is a product of what men have chosen to do with their power over women and their words.

Jean Baker Miller has noted that 'A dominant group, inevitably, has the greatest influence in determining a culture's overall outlook . . .' (Miller, 1977, p. 8) and in our society we can easily see why this is so. As the dominant group, men are seen, currently and historically, as the authority on social, economic and political issues. They have also had access to the resources to enforce their authority and provide them with recognizable power. Beyond this, however, men have been in positions to impose sanctions against women who have been perceived as posing some sort of threat or challenge to male supremacy. Thus women who have made significant cultural contributions have had to be dealt with by men. Whether women's challenge to men has lain in their insistence on an alternative and equally valid realm of experience to the alleged universal experience of men, or in achievement at a level usually reserved for men, men have been obliged to react in order to preserve the existing power structures. To maintain the male-as-dominant norm and to preserve the notion of male authority, men have had to discredit the autonomous voices of women or, in more gentlemanly fashion, to ensure that the positive reputations of the women and their work have enjoyed only a limited life-span.

In our society this has not been a difficult task. Our social, political and economic arrangements involve women's dependence on men and place women in positions where qualifying for male approval on both a personal and professional level becomes a major consideration. The arrangements simultaneously place men in positions where their witholding of approval, or their outright imposition of sanctions against disobedient women, can have far-reaching effects on women's aspirations and achievements. Men are also in a position to rationalize their actions as normal and justifiable.

The development of this situation is perfectly understandable from a male point of view and clearly recognizable from a feminist point of view. The only alternative available to men has been to acknowledge the validity of female experience and female knowledge. Such an alternative would have required men to admit that their decisions and solutions have not always been the most appropriate ones and that certain issues which men have considered marginal (child-care for example) are absolutely central, when the experience of the entire population is taken into account. In effect, acknowledgment of the validity of women's experience would have required men to relinquish their traditional privilege of claiming sole authority on all 'important' issues and to recognize the artificial basis of their superiority. It would disturb the arrangements that have allowed men to exist in the manner to which they have become accustomed.

Not surprisingly, men have shown a reluctance to voluntarily relinquish any of their acquired privileges. In fact they have made concerted efforts to retain them at women's expense. The result has been that our received tradition in every area where men have been responsible for the selection of material for inclusion within our culture is likely to reflect men's fears and reveal the subsequent harassment of women who have quickened those fears. Thus in literature, the arts, science, religion and the law, our published heritage is not merely an accumulation of ideas and knowledge, dispassionately recorded and attributed to their original source. It has a specific political component which reflects the power configurations of our male-dominated society and omits mention of the sorts of harassment that have been practised on those who have challenged male control. For example, not a great deal of research is required to go beyond the explanations provided in male-recorded histories and to make connections between the hysterical witch hunts of the fifteenth, sixteenth and seventeenth centuries and a male fear of female knowledge and power. Nor does it involve a huge imaginative leap to associate the same sort of fear with the deliberate appropriation of the practice of medicine by the new breed of male experts during the nineteenth century. Control of reproduction especially was a far too important area to remain within the hands of women, so female midwives were persecuted and harassed while male practitioners, often with no knowledge at all of childbirth, assumed control of reproduction (Ehrenreich and English, 1979). Even the most naïve of us could not today accept that the outlawing of female midwifery in many Western societies is adequately explained by sheer altruistic concern for the welfare of mothers and children.

Indeed, in almost every area where social and cultural norms are ordained (and of which publishing is definitely one) there is evidence of the harassment of women who have come close to the established centres of male power and whose knowledge has appeared threatening. In their book *Sexism and the Law* (1978), Sachs and Hoff Wilson document the wheeling and dealing, the manipulation and harassment in which our revered legal fathers indulged in order to exclude women from recognition in any capacity within the legal framework. Time and again, the male makers and interpreters of the law resisted women's knowledge about women and instead chose to use the knowledge about women provided by other men – knowledge which served to protect the male monopoly over property, personhood and power.

In art, as Linda Nochlin pointed out in 1971, 'things as they are and as they have been in the arts, as in a hundred other areas, are stultifying, oppressive and discouraging to all who did not have the good fortune to be born white, preferably middle-class or above, males' (Nochlin, 1971, p. 483). More recently Germaine Greer, in referring to the condescending attitudes (a more 'polite' manifestation of harassment) exhibited by commentators on art, stated 'any work by a woman, however trifling, is as astonishing as the pearl in the head of the toad. It is not part of the natural order, and need not be related to the natural order' (Greer, 1979, p. 4). The harassment of women embodied in the denial of the existence of women within the 'natural order' requires little elaboration, at least among women.

In science the situation is just as revealing about the roles played by sexual harassment and male approval in the entrance of women into the field and in the recognition of women's scientific contributions to our culture. On many occasions, women who earned reputations in their own time as learned scholars have since been edited out of the records of scientific achievement. How many of us, for example, have heard of Aspasia, whom Rita Arditti describes as 'the most learned woman in the ancient world (whom Socrates called "my teacher" and who is credited with writing the best speeches of Pericles)' (Arditti, 1980, p. 351)? The theory of gatekeeping based on male approval suggests that her absence from the records may be attributable not only to her usurpation of a male domain but because 'She criticised the institution of marriage as it existed in Athens and tried to educate Athenian women and men about the need for equality of the sexes' (p. 351). It is understandable that such knowledge was not welcomed and that Aspasia's contributions to science and society were ushered into obscurity.

There are other significant and similar examples of the refusal of men to acknowledge the contributions of women to science. Hypatia of Alexandra (A.D. 370–415), who among other achievements 'invented an astrolabe and a plane-sphere, an apparatus for distilling water, another for

determining the specific gravity of liquids and one for determining the level of water' is not recognized as a major figure
in the history of science. References to her emphasize her
death at the hands of a mob of religious fanatics rather than
her work, and 'the fact that she was a brilliant mathe-
matician is relegated to the background' (Arditti, p. 352).
Hypatia's sex and not her work has emerged as her salient
feature.

Within this century Madame Curie, although one of the
few women whose names are associated with major contributions to science, met with a share of male disapproval and
harassment. She was denied membership to the French
Academy of Science where membership was recognized in the
scientific community as 'proof of scientific ability'. Similarly,
Maria Gaetana Agnesi and Sophie Germain, who also won
wide reputations for their work, were never allowed official
membership to the Academy because 'La tradition ne veut
pas d'academici*ennes*' (Arditti, p. 355 – my emphasis). This
blatant harassment of women because of their sex and the
ease with which their exclusion from the Academy allowed
the appropriation of their work without the need to acknowledge the women themselves, or their ability, has contributed
to the invisibility of women as creative people. At the same
time it has conveniently reserved for men the reputation of
scientific ability.

Another more recent example of the operation of a
system based on male approval concerns the scientific work of
Rosalind Franklin. There seems little doubt in the minds of
those who have studied her work that she 'was the first to
establish the helical structure of DNA' (Arditti, p. 359), but
credit for the discovery has consistently been given to her
male colleagues. Both they and the history of science record
the discovery without acknowledging Franklin's real contribution. (See also Hubbard, 1979, pp. 261–73.)

In literature, too, there is a great deal of evidence to show
that whenever women's words and knowledge have dealt
with areas outside male experience or have threatened male
control, men have resisted their entry into the literary
records. Louise Bernikow explains that 'male approval, the
poet's condition of survival, is withheld when a woman

shapes her poetry from the very material that contradicts or threatens male reality' (Bernikow, 1974, p. 7). The approval has been withheld from many women writers who have been regarded as social deviants and it has been withheld from their work by the institution of publishing which has been at liberty to select and choose only the material of which it has approved.

Women writers, from the time they dared to circulate their work publicly, have been subjected to harassment from men for entering male territory and for allegedly denying their male-defined femininity. They have had to contend with the imposition of limitations to their education, to their opportunities to write and to their chances to publish and circulate their work. Even after their words have been printed, women have had to face male literary criticism in order to determine the fate of their work. In each case and at each stage women have been pressured to conform to men's requirements to meet with male approval. There is quite a credible argument that one of the most consistent traditions associated with women's writing is the sexual harassment to which its authors have been exposed when they have attempted to join men in the literary world.

In order to write, women require some education. They need to be literate, and we know that until fairly recently in our society women were often denied that opportunity. Men, in their role as determiners of social policy, were within their rights to decree, as some of them still do today, that an education was wasted on women. Even when it was accepted in Western societies that women should receive formal schooling, men had no concept that it should be the same sort of education that prepared men for their roles in the public world. Instead, women's education was intended to provide women with the skills and charms that would make them better wives and mothers. They were to be educated according to the male notion of the ideal woman – one who would support man in his public role while herself remaining silent and confined to the private world.

Universities did not consider themselves obliged to admit women students until the nineteenth century and then in some instances imposed conditions whereby women were permitted to study only if they did not graduate or practise their profession in opposition to men. The now documented trials of women like Sophia Jex-Blake, Elizabeth Garrett and many others (Kamm, 1966) and the physical as well as psychological harassment that these women experienced provide awful evidence of the lengths to which many men were prepared to go to exclude women from what they saw as male prerogatives.

Today there is evidence to show that female students still do not have access to the same education as their male counterparts. The pattern of male dominance exists in the classrooms where harassment of female students and teachers is considered normal (Spender; 1982b). It exists in universities where male students are sponsored and channelled into career paths and where staff hierarchies generally place tenured men in the top positions and women, untenured and part-time, at the bottom. It also exists in the organizational structures where educational policy is decided and where there is a definite correlation between being male and being in the more prestigious and powerful positions. In 1978 in England, men made up 97 per cent of the 'government of education' (Byrne, 1978, p. 15). At the same time in Canada it was shown that women were 'markedly underrepresented in administrative positions and positions of professional leadership' and that generally 'power and authority in the educational process are the prerogatives of men' (Smith, 1978, p. 289). A similar situation exists in Australia where 'senior positions at school and tertiary levels are almost completely male territory' (Roper, 1975, p. 117). In the past this sort of educational gatekeeping has disadvantaged women who wished to write. Deprived of an education comparable to that of their brothers, women were freely and even 'gleefully' criticized by the educated male establishment when evidence of inferior scholarship or intellectual pretension could be identified in their work (Showalter, 1971, p. 41). In other words women were harassed then as they are now when they compete with men. The only difference today is that women are now told (and frequently believe) that they have the same educational opportunities as their brothers, in spite of convincing empirical evidence to the contrary (Spender, 1982b).

Apart from the qualitative and quantitative differences in their education from that of men, women have had to write within a culture that has for centuries seen them as inferior beings and one where literary creativity has been seen as a peculiarly male characteristic (Gilbert and Gubar, 1979). Under these circumstances women writers have been criticized for 'stealing' from men. The right to write and receive public recognition for achievement has been freely granted only to men, while women have had to struggle continually to earn it. St Paul is recorded as advocating that 'women learn in silence and with all subjection' and the idea that women's voices should not be heard in a public context (which is what publishing makes possible) has not altered very much. Recently Norman Mailer insisted that 'balls' were a prerequisite for good writing and the notion of 'literary paternity' (Gilbert and Gubar, 1979) whereby men 'father' the written word and then own it, allows no more space for women's literary autonomy than does the practice of social paternity whereby women are 'owned' by their fathers and 'given away' to be owned by their husbands.

Of course women have been allowed to write material of which men have approved and that has usually been the ideas and the forms which have reinforced women's confinement to the private world. Journals, diaries and letters to maintain essential family and social communications have been permitted when they have in no way challenged men's control of public communication. 'Letters,' said Virginia Woolf, 'did not count. A woman might write letters while she was sitting by her father's sick-bed. She could write them by the fire whilst the men talked without disturbing them' (Woolf, 1977, p. 60). Treatises and domestic advice to other women, when they affirmed women's traditional roles, have been seen as appropriate contributions to our written heritage and have sometimes even survived as quaint reminders of the good old days. After publishing became a commercial proposition and women showed themselves willing and able to write the triple-decker novels of the eighteenth and nineteenth centuries, publishers were not loath to engage women writers. The subscription method of publishing, whereby all costs of publication and most of the

profits were collected before the books were issued, assured
publishers of a satisfactory deal. The sale of copyright to
publishers for a flat sum left the less assertive women writers
with a less satisfactory deal. Showalter points out that it
'left authors dependent on the goodwill of publishers, and
often put women authors in the role of supplicant; the copyright system kept even successful writers at the grindstone
of constant production' (Showalter, 1978, p. 50). As Virginia
Woolf remarked of Mrs Oliphant, and it was no doubt true
of many other women writers, the demands of publishers
and women's need to earn a living did not lead to 'dis-
interested culture and intellectual liberty' (Woolf 1977b, p.
166). Today, for the same commercial reasons, women are
perfectly acceptable as writers of Harlequin-type romances
and it is not insignificant that many of the three-deckers and
most of the Harlequins affirm that women's ultimate
happiness and fulfilment depend on their finally catching – a
man!

However, the salvage work done by women like Elaine
Showalter, Ellen Moers, Joan Goulianos, Louise Bernikow,
Virginia Woolf and Dale Spender shows us that the same
acceptability has not been associated with women's writing
when it has confounded the public/private dichotomy established by men. When women have presented feminist sentiments in the public world and have dealt with matters of
public (that is, male) concern, they have met with patterns of
male resistance aimed at undermining their personal credibility and that of their work. They have met with various
forms of *sexual harassment*.

The list of women who have received negative treatment
at the hands and pens of the male literary establishment is
already long and as more is discovered about 'lost' women
writers, it continues to grow. It includes Margery Kempe
from the fourteenth century, Jane Anger from the sixteenth
century, Margaret Cavendish, Anne Finch, Aphra Behn
and Anne Bradstreet in the seventeenth century, Mary
Wollstonecraft and Lady Mary Wortley Montague in the
eighteenth century, Harriet Martineau, Emily Dickinson
and many others in the nineteenth century and in our own
time Germaine Greer, Kate Millett and Mary Daly – women

writers who have ventured into the public arena have all been subjected to expressions of male disapproval. They have become prime candidates to qualify for inclusion in a heritage which sooner or later, with men in control, will no doubt become 'unpublished'. Men are aware that the autonomous voices of women present a threat to male security. They know that women who operate outside the boundaries of male approval may form an independent female tradition in direct opposition to the male as dominant tradition. We as women know that of opposition and subversion, men do not approve!

Joan Goulianos contends that whenever women have written to express their own understandings of their world and their lives, they have done so in a hostile environment. Of the women dealt with in *By A Woman Writt* (1974), Goulianos claims,

> they wrote in a world which was controlled by men, a
> world in which women's revelations, if they were
> anything but conventional might not be welcomed,
> might not be recognized . . . Their writings were . . . not
> only 'literature', but acts of courage. (p. xiv)

Yet they did write and we now have information going back to the sixteenth century about certain women, who by virtue of privilege, money and family connections (not to mention dire necessity) managed to acquire an education and access to the literary world. In reconstructing their past and ours, we are becoming aware of the consistent and systematic exclusion of their work from the mainstream of our literary heritage. We are also beginning to understand the harassment of women that this has involved and the reasons for its practice.

Mary Sidney Herbert (1561–1621), Countess of Pembroke, was exposed through her father and brother to 'the world of letters'. She was permitted to participate in it by providing a salon for the meeting of literary people and to sponsor young and aspiring (male) writers. She also wrote – but what has been selected for posterity from her writing is the 'editing' of her brother's work, a translation of the Psalms and an elegy to her brother on his death. Nothing of her autonomous voice remains. Her epitaph, which describes her as 'Sidney's sister, Pembroke's mother' is an indication of the contribution literary ladies were apparently expected to make (Bernikow, 1974, p. 53).

Later into the seventeenth century, other privileged women stepped outside the public/private classification that guarded literary and social traditions but they were obviously aware of the established 'property rights' they violated and the censure they risked. Wisely no doubt, they covered their trespass with apologies and explanations. Outside the elite and controlled literary enclaves it was considered a 'violation of morality and a ruination of virtue for a woman to write and present her work to a public audience' (Bernikow, 1974, p. 18). In a society where a woman's virtue was one of her few assets, such a standard represented both implicit and explicit limitations on women's personal and literary aspirations. If women wanted men's approval – and most needed it in order to survive – they were to remain silent. They 'knew quite well that if one woman signed her work with her own name, she opened herself to social and moral abuse' (p. 20).

Thus when the first volume of the poems of Katherine Philips was published in the seventeenth century, ostensibly without her knowledge, she claimed, 'she who never writ any line in my life with intention to have it printed. . . . I did not so much resist it as a wiser women would have done' (quoted in Bernikow, pp. 22–3). Writing under the pseudonym 'Orinda' and referred to in her time as the 'English Sappho' (p. 58), she established a considerable reputation as a literary personality. Like Mary Sidney she organized a literary salon that included several prominent men and like Mary, she too translated work into English. Apparently the translation of men's work was seen as no threat to *male* creativity. Her poetry consciously removed itself from public, male themes and did not challenge male ownership of important issues. She is even alleged to have stated that 'submissive greatness' was the 'modest woman's rightful place in history' (p. 39).

But 'Orinda' has not survived as the English Sappho, nor has she achieved submissive greatness in our literary heritage. When she has been considered at all by critics and commentators, they have overlooked her writing about 'love and women, often both together . . . knowing less what to say about it than the critics used to know what to say of Shakespeare's love for the young man' (p. 23). Her perceptions and understandings have obviously not seemed important to the gatekeepers and except where she is dealt with in feminist studies, her contributions to literature have been removed.

It seems fairly significant that neither 'Orinda', who apparently conformed to male-approved standards, nor Mary Sidney who apparently ignored them, has been allowed to survive as a literary personality. Regardless of the approach adopted by the women, men have still managed to impose their standards and their power of veto, and in doing so have indicated the breadth and pervasiveness of their techniques of control.

With the poetry of Anne Finch (1661–1720), Countess of Winchilsea, the line of male approval drawn between the public world of men and the private world of women was dramatically named and exposed.

Aware of the prejudice, if not contempt, to which she would be subjected, Anne Finch published her first poems anonymously. Many of them dealt with the problems of the 'woman that attempts the pen,/Such an intruder on the rights of men'. They specifically named the patriarchal notion of literature as a male domain and the 'dull manage of a servile house' as woman's proper place. Her sentiments still carry a remarkably familiar ring as do the penalties that women will pay if they provoke male disapproval:

> To write, or read, or think, or to enquire
> Wou'd cloud our beauty, and exhaust our time,
>   (Anne Finch, quoted in Goulianos, 1974, p. 71)

Needless to say, the poems of Anne Finch, dependent as they were on male approval for success, did not enter the hallowed halls of literary fame. How different it may have been if women had been selecting the 'best' work available. Women today have joyously celebrated Finch's work for its style and relevance to their own lives. Dilys Laing (1906–1960) replied to Anne Finch,

Staunch Anne! I know your trouble. The same tether
galls us. To be a woman and a writer
is double mischief, for the world will slight her
who slights 'the servile house', and who would rather
make odes than beds. Lost lady! Gentle fighter!
Separate in time, we mutiny together. (Dilys Laing,
quoted in Goulianos, 1974, p. 329)

And so it goes on!

Margaret Cavendish (1623–1673), Duchess of
Newcastle, whose writing reflected her belief in creativity
and innovation – 'there is more pleasure in making than in
mending' – Woolf, 1979, p. 83) was anathema to the literary
critics who harassed her by ridiculing her work and herself as
'Mad Madge'. Her poems, plays, discourses, orations and
philosophies 'moulder in the gloom of public libraries. . . .'
(Woolf, 1979, p. 79). If she is included at all today in literary
circles outside specifically feminist ones, it is for her
biography of her husband. As with Mary Sidney, all that is
left, all that has met with male approval, is a tribute to a male
literary figure.

Into what was still a male-dominated and fairly closed
literary environment in the seventeenth century, entered
Aphra Behn (c. 1640–1689). Her impact on the world of
letters and the threat that she posed to it can be gauged by the
bitterness and frequency of the attacks made upon her. Not
only did Aphra Behn cross the line which divided the private
and public worlds, she earned a living from doing so and,
according to Virginia Woolf, earned all women 'the right to
speak their minds' (Woolf, 1979, p. 91). The fierce resentment
that accompanied her visible success as a playwright was
voiced in misogynic poems about her and in the 'invective and
character assassination from the self-appointed critics who
still assembled after the play to make or break its "fame" in
the town' (Goreau, 1980, p. 263). The abuse and harassment
centred on her sex rather than her work and the scandalous
reputation she acquired undoubtedly contributed to her
exclusion from the literary mainstream. She was identified
as being fifty years ahead of her time in her radical belief in
the rights of human beings to act according to their

conscience (an idea attributed to Rousseau fifty years later) and there is evidence to show that even in male-defined terms, her fiction qualified as the first 'novels' long before Richardson and Defoe had written theirs.

But Aphra has disappeared and it does not take more than one reading of her work to see why. Far from earning male approval, Aphra Behn must have repulsed it. She refused to stay within the confines of the female literary subculture as it had been defined by men and insisted on writing scathing criticisms of the male-dominated society and its institutions. Her first play, *The Forced Marriage* (1671), dealt with the destructive effects of the social practice of marriage during her time – hardly an appropriate topic for any woman, let alone one with access to a huge public audience. Her poem 'The Disappointment', a delightful account (from a female point of view) of an amorous but impotent male, must have received a less than joyful reception from the men who had never before had the sanctity of their private lives invaded in such an amusing (to women) and public way. Her complete excision from the male-determined literary tradition is understandable, from a male point of view. To even contemplate a tradition arising from Aphra Behn's work must have been enough to send men scurrying to their gatekeeping posts to ensure that nothing of Behn's work survived and that such a mistake could not be made again. To a certain extent, they suceeded. Aphra Behn constitutes a prime example of what Germaine Greer referred to as 'the phenomena of the transience of literary fame', (Greer, 1974), whereby women who have enjoyed success and fame during their own lifetimes have been rendered invisible in the generations that followed. Their invisibility, as we know now, is far from arbitrary. It is a direct result of males effecting gatekeeping and harassment in order to prevent challenges or changes to the standards of their own literary and social existence.

By the eighteenth century, women moving into the world of literature were not confined to those in exceptional circumstances. For a variety of reasons, not the least of which was the growth of publishing as a commercial venture, women began to be published in greater numbers, especially when they wrote what men saw as appropriate. But they were no more to be considered part of the literary mainstream than individuals like Mary Manley (c. 1663–1724), who made a visible impact (in her own time) on the world of letters.

Mary Manley stepped way outside the prescribed boundaries for women by becoming perhaps England's first female political journalist. Her feminist and satirical writings which dealt openly and effectively with 'male' issues apparently caused sufficient stir (she was at one stage arrested for her writing), to justify her disappearance from the generations to follow (Goulianos, 1974, p. 103). The existence of such a female, acknowledged in the historical records, is not in the interests of men who wish to preserve their view of the world as the legitimate one. A role model such as Mary Manley must have been perceived as quite threatening. What other explanation is there for her excision from the history of publishing and publishers?

It is not difficult to see, with hindsight, why, when Mary Wollstonecraft appeared on the public literary scene, her fate closely paralleled that of Aphra Behn one hundred years earlier. Mary Wollstonecraft (1759–1797) was also a 'woman of ideas' (Spender, 1982a). She not only wrote publicly but ignored that standard that expected her to remain within the traditional female sphere. She wrote in a way openly critical of social mores and values and suffered the inevitable consequences. Her book *A Vindication of the Rights of Woman*, a feminist declaration of independence, brought a response which today can be seen as an expression of fear on the part of those who had most to lose by the principles she espoused. Wollstonecraft made the connection two hundred years ago between women's 'inferiority' and the convenience for the dominant male group of having a ready-made inferior class; she recognized the relationship between the socializing processes that were arranged for women and their disadvantaged position in society. Horace Walpole called her 'a hyena in petticoats' and refused to read her work, as did a number of literary ladies who thought her too extreme. *Historical Magazine* gave an indication of the reception given to *A Vindication* by suggesting that it be read

> with disgust by every female who has any pretensions to delicacy; with detestation by every one attached to the interests of religion and morality, and with indignation by anyone who might feel any regard for the unhappy woman, whose frailties should have been buried in oblivion. (quoted in Kramnick, 1975, p. 8)

All the penalties previously brought out by men to prevent subversive doctrines from reaching a wide audience were used against Mary Wollstonecraft. There was no reasonable rebuttal of the principle she put forward. There was no attempt to debate the issues she raised. Instead she was abused, vilified and ridiculed. Her personal life, her personality, her relationships, her moral integrity and her intellectual integrity were all maligned. She was refused acknowledgment during her time as a 'learned' woman and has since been cast in the mould of the man-hating woman, an image which has become the stereotypical version of the feminist woman whenever she has threatened man's superior position (Kramnick, 1975, p. 7).

Today, not in history, literature, law or philosophy are Mary Wollstonecraft and her ideas addressed. It is ironical to realize that if her work had been accepted, if the feminist principles she espoused had been allowed to circulate and survive, the effort that has gone into recovering her work and that of other 'lost' feminist writers could well have gone into pressing for the principle to be put into practice. Cunning, isn't it?

The phenomenon of the 'bluestocking' in the late eighteenth century, seemingly belied the dictum that women should have no autonomous or visible place in English literary society. The women of 'hi-lit' taste who became known as 'bluestockings' participated in and even led much of the literary activity in the latter half of the eighteenth century. It was apparently not their intent to forge a new role for a new acceptance for women as writers or to challenge men in the public world, but in several ways they did provide a foundation for women's images of themselves to expand. By publishing their own books and articles and bypassing the male press (only because they had the money and connections to do so), the bluestockings established that women were perfectly competent to perform 'male' literary activities. They were not regarded by all with the respect that they may have wanted. Horace Walpole, although hardly an advocate for women with ideas, commented that 'They vie with one another till they are as intelligible as the good folks at Babel' (Manley and Belcher, 1972, p. 62), which may well have been another gatekeeping and harassing comment. They were heard though – or he would not have felt obliged to respond to their 'babble'. Their partial appropriation of the gatekeeping of their own work was sufficient to warrant the intervention of the male gatekeepers, and by the end of the century the term 'bluestockings', which had previously been associated with wit, intelligence and society, had come to be ridiculed and to be associated with pedantry. Little of their contribution remains in our literary records, but Mr Boswell's comment about them has been preserved. According to this gentleman, their salons were places where 'the fair sex . . . animated by a desire to please . . . might participate in conversation with literary and ingenious men' (Manley and Belcher, 1972, p. 62). The image of coquettish, female admirers of great men emerges and the traditionally approved concept of the female literary role is carefully preserved.

Fanny Burney (1752–1840), closely associated with the bluestockings and since acknowledged by Virginia Woolf as 'the mother of English fiction' (Woolf, 1979, p. 69), faded from literary significance along with them. Fanny Burney also experienced forms of harassment familiar to other female writers. Her writing was done without the approval of her father and initially without his knowledge. Her stepmother at one stage ordered that all her manuscripts be burned (Woolf, 1979, p. 69). Her home was considered a fairly Bohemian one at the time, but Bohemianism did not include tolerance for women as writers and Fanny was afraid to write openly: 'The fear of discovery or suspicion in the house made the copying extremely laborious for me. . . . I was obliged to stay up the greatest part of my night to get it ready' (Quoted in Manley and Belcher, 1972).

What was finally ready was an epistolary novel, *Evelina*,

the story of a young woman's entrance into London society. It was immediately successful and according to Austin Dobson in the Introduction to the 1903 edition, it was 'the most popular novel which had appeared for a considerable time, having probably a larger number of educated readers than Goldsmith's *Vicar of Wakefield* (Dobson, Introduction to *Evelina*, 1903). Yet sixty years later another male critic judged Fanny Burney as having had only 'a tenuous store of invention to support her own observation and experience' in contrast to the contemporary male novelist Samuel Richardson who 'could create' (Evans, 1963, p. 167)! Burney's first play, *The Witlings*, described by Ellen Moers as 'very funny and quite stageworthy' (1977, p. 177) reached no further than manuscript stage. Her father prevented its public presentation for fear that it may have upset the literary women whom it so cleverly satirized. And well it may have done, but it may also have made a significant contribution to our subsequent literary traditions, especially the female tradition. No one I think convinced Pope or Shaw, or for that matter any male satirist, that their work should not be published for fear of disturbing the people or conventions that were the butt of their satire. No one I think harassed Dryden or Swift for indulging in personal criticism. Instead their work has been elevated to a literary genre and countless students have looked to them as (male) models. Meanwhile, Fanny Burney's work has been hidden away and her reputation set into decline. The only consolation, and a rather negative one, is that even if Fanny Burney's play had been publicly presented and proved popular or clever, it would probably still only be available to those few interested readers who have traced it to its resting place in the New York Public Library (Moers, 1977, p. 177). Seven more plays were written by Fanny Burney during her lifetime, none of them published, although her last comedy, *A Busy Day*, has been referred to as an 'unpublished masterpiece' (Moers, 1977 p. 178). If male gatekeeping and sexual harassment can engineer this, then the dominant group can engineer anything.

But of course it has not been just 'anything' that has been engineered. What has been effectively devised and efficiently carried out is a system that men have used to maintain their dominant role in literature as in the rest of society. By the end of the eighteenth century, the patterns that were to dictate literary tradition had been set. By disparaging women and their literary output when they did not meet with male approval, the gatekeepers had established that there was to be little rational connection between merit – as reflected by the popularity and success of women's work among contemporary readers – and the subsequent placing of women within the literary tradition. The myth of male supremacy in literature and in life was still intact and the techniques of harassment of women who ventured into competition with men through treating writing as work were established as part of our cultural heritage.

Chapter 5

Success by Default

Halfway through the nineteenth century, Mrs Oliphant, a woman of considerable literary reputation, declared that the century was 'the age of female novelists' (Showalter, 1978, p. 75). It is easy to see that she was referring to the number of successful novels, written by women, which seemed to have inundated the literary market. Yet, looking back from the perspective provided in this century, it is also easy to see that the concessions that were granted to women as writers and which allowed them to earn this praise were given more by default than by a change in the traditional line that had previously dictated that women play a minor role in the literary world.

The century began with Jane Austen writing novels on the manners and morals of the gentry – in isolation, obscurity and anonymity. Her first novel appeared as written by 'A Lady', and apparently the 'lady' did not initially take the literary scene by storm as some of her predecessors had done. There is an argument that her inclusion in the literary canons came much later and that she was selected as a 'great' novelist, not just for her scenes of country life with their gentle and subtle irony and her skills in social analysis and character portrayal, but because her work had the added quality of qualifying as 'women's writing' and thus posed little threat to the mainstream, male tradition. Jane Austen could be allowed to emerge from the nineteenth century as a great writer and occupy a special place in the literary hierarchy providing it was not a place that challenged the supremacy of 'real' male writing. Her inclusion in the records in a position just slightly removed from male writers may throw light on the question of why any women at all have been included in literary history. Accepting and acknowledging Jane Austen's work, the literary establishment may have felt perfectly justified in then rejecting the more subversive material presented by her peers.

Other women who were published during the early part of the nineteenth century were obviously still very aware of the disapproval they might encounter by assuming public identities. The Brontës, who after many rejections finally had their work published under the male pseudonyms of Currer, Ellis and Acton Bell, were conscious that 'authoresses are liable to be looked on with prejudice' (Charlotte Brontë, quoted in Showalter, 1978, p. 59). Showalter describes the common use of the male pseudonym as a signal of 'the loss of innocence' by female writers in its 'radical understanding of the role-playing required by women's effort to participate in the mainstream of literary culture' (1978, p. 19). Women became aware that their chances for publication were not based on 'merit' alone. Social expectations and commercial considerations played a large part in women's attempts at writing and in publishers' willingness to accept their work. Publishers themselves recommended the use of male pseudonyms if they thought the books would stand a better chance of success when presented as the work of a man (Showalter, 1978, p. 59).

Women journalists writing at the time frequently presented their articles unsigned – as did many male journalists – but women also assumed a male 'persona' or a 'mannish' way of talking when they dealt with worldly (male) issues. Showalter quotes George Eliot in this context as saying of an article that she had written for the *Westminster*, 'The article appears to have produced a strong impression, and that impression would be a little counteracted if the author were known to be a woman' (George Eliot, quoted in Showalter, 1978, p. 60).

Whether she was aware that resentment of her usurpation of a male prerogative may have been involved as well as the usual practice of devaluing women's ideas is not clear. But certainly George Eliot's name and her comment indicate that she recognized that for men, women and writing did not sit comfortably together.

Harriet Martineau, one of the journalists referred to as 'mannish' in her way of talking in print (Showalter, 1978, p. 59) wrote a fictionalized account of economics in order to make the subject more accessible to more people. Entitled *Illustration of Political Economy*, the book was rejected by publisher after publisher and, as its popularity after it was finally accepted and printed showed, the initial rejections cannot have been based on an accurate assessment of the demand for the book. A clue to its rejection and the rejection of more of her work even after she became an established writer may well be contained in her own words in 1832: 'I want to be doing something with the pen, since no other means of action in politics are in a woman's power' (Moers, 1977, p. 30). The record of her travels to the Middle East – *Eastern Life, Past and Present* also found publishers reluctant to accept it, yet it too was highly acclaimed when it appeared. Perhaps there may have been more than a little significance in the fact that her view of the harem 'contrasts strikingly with the romanticised picture that male writers often give' (Goulianos, 1974, p. 199).

Women also had the feeling, as they did in the sixteenth century, that the sort of notoriety and publicity that came with being a public figure was undesirable. Many women writers expressed fears similar to those of Mary Brunton who claimed that she preferred anonymity to being noticed, and commented on and 'shunned as literary women are, by the more unpretending of my own sex' (Showalter, 1977, p. 17). And there is no doubt that their fears were well founded. The reactions to Charlotte Brontë's *Jane Eyre* and to George Eliot's *Adam Bede* clearly demonstrated this.

Initially well received when issued under male pseudonyms. *Adam Bede* and *Jane Eyre* brought outcries from the critics when it was discovered that they were written by women. The cries were not expressions of delight that women were capable of writing 'great' novels. They were cries of objection that Charlotte Brontë and George Eliot were 'unfeminine'. Rather than providing evidence that it was time for the traditional and limiting expectations of women's writing to change, it signalled men to tighten the restrictions and put women in their place. Charlotte Brontë's lack of 'taste' was associated with her exposure to foreign influences during her trip to Brussels and George Eliot's was attributed to her immoral lifestyle. She was after all, 'living' with G. H. Lewes and critics had few qualms about implying that the relationship coloured her work in more ways than one. *Adam Bede* fell from being regarded as 'too good for a woman's story' to being seen as 'a tale with no great quality of any kind' (Showalter, 1978, p. 94). Even the old standby of undermining women's scholarship was tried when *The Quarterly* criticized its 'classical quotations', which as George Eliot herself pointed out was quite erroneous as in all her novels there was only one classical quotation (Showalter 1978, p. 95).

So while it may be that women were established as novelists during the nineteenth century, it was not necessarily because of a new acceptance of women as equals in terms of their creative potential in the literary world. The exaggerated and hostile reaction of many critics and male writers to their domain being invaded by 'women, children and ill-trained troops' (G. H. Lewes, 1847, quoted in Showalter, 1978, p. 39) indicates that women's new place was by no means approved of or applauded by all. That there was no correlation between their acceptance as writers of novels and as writers of other forms of literature seems to show that the popularity of the novel and women's ability and desire to write it may have taken the literary world and its gatekeepers by surprise.

Men had established themselves as the 'arbiters of . . . convention' (Woolf, 1979, p. 49) in life and literature, but the novel as a literary form was new. There were no established precedents and no 'objective' male standards by which men could judge women's novel-writing as inferior. The commercial possibilities that the increasing numbers of women readers and writers seemed to promise may have made the gatekeepers careless, for by the time a new convention of women as novelists was established, the 'invasion' had taken place. Men were obliged to allow women a place. All they could do was watch and criticize from the sidelines in the hope that the penalties that had worked against women in the past to minimize their contributions would again prove sufficient eventually to leave the literary tradition unpolluted.

Feminist research into the lives and work of nineteenth-century women writers shows that generally this is what did happen. With the exception of the few acknowledged 'greats', the lives and works of other women from the time have been eclipsed. Elizabeth Barrett Browning, for example, has been reduced in stature from the poet who was a major candidate for the *Poet Laureateship* to one who has been all but totally excised from our literary heritage. Today, as in 1932 when Virginia Woolf said 'Nobody reads her, nobody discusses her, nobody troubles to put her in her place' (Woolf, 1979, p. 134), we realize that even her 'place' has been removed. My own studies of English literature, both undergraduate and post-graduate, did not acknowledge Elizabeth Barrett for any more than two of her traditional and romantic *Sonnets of the Portuguese* ('How do I love thee?' and 'When two souls stand erect'). As far as I knew this was her contribution to English literature, or at least constituted her 'best' work. I had no idea that she had been passionately interested in social and political questions and that she had written *Aurora Leigh*, the epic poem which dealt specifically with the 'woman question' in its study of the development of a woman writer. I wonder, as others have done, what difference it would have made to me as a female student of literature to have studied *Aurora Leigh* instead of *Portrait of the Artist as a Young Man*!

Cora Kaplan, in her Introduction to the 1978 edition of *Aurora Leigh* (The Women's Press), the first full-length edition of the poem for over seventy years, offers some interesting insights into its treatment as a contribution to our literary history. Her observations are not inconsistent with my own thesis about gatekeeping and the importance of male approval. Kaplan identifies the 'taboo' against women's entry into public discourse as speakers and writers and suggests that the male-dominated ruling class had reason to think that the taboo was in danger of being broken during the nineteenth century. One of the ways to prevent that from happening was to exert even tighter control over established economic, social and political conventions. She says,

> In an age characterised by the importance of the popular press as the place of ideological production and the spread of female literacy, it was of prime importance to warn women off questioning traditonal sexual morality. (Kaplan, 1978, p. 9)

Much of Elizabeth Barrett Browning's work questioned more than just sexual morality, although that was the focal point of criticism of *Aurora Leigh*. In spite of its tremendous popularity – it went into a second edition within two weeks of its initial publication – Blackwoods felt obliged to comment that 'The extreme independence of Aurora detracts from the feminine charm, and mars the interest which we otherwise might have felt in so intellectual a heroine' (quoted in Kaplan, p. 13). Reverting to techniques used effectively in the past to silence 'uppity' women, the *Dublin University Review* stated,

> Indeed in the effort to stand, not only on a pedestal beside man, but actually to occupy his place, we see Mrs Browning commit grave errors. . . . She is occasionally coarse in expression and unfeminine in thought; and utters what, if they be even truths, are so conveyed that we would hesitate to present them to the eye of the readers of her own sex. . . . The days when such a woman as Aphra Behn can hope to be palatable to the female sex are gone forever. (quoted in Kaplan, 1978, p. 13)

The 'arrangements' are familiar and we become aware that Elizabeth Barrett Browning's *Aurora Leigh* must have seemed extremely threatening to those who guarded the literary bastions. The idea of a woman writing about a woman writing offers a legitimacy for women as writers that men have not wanted them to have. If, like Elizabeth Barrett Browning, they write love sonnets (heterosexual), then they may receive acknowledgment, but if they challenge the prevailing 'truths' as she did with *Aurora Leigh* and disturb the traditional power structures, they can expect the full force of male defence mechanisms to come into action. If one or two trick their way in, as did George Eliot and Charlotte Brontë, they can be explained and even allowed to survive as examples of a special (and inferior) category of female literature or, altenatively, as 'women possessed of the proper masculine power of writing books' (Coventry Patmore quoted in Showalter, 1978, p. 75). But men have made it quite clear that they would prefer no general acceptance of women as creative equals within the patriarchal-literary tradition.

By the end of the nineteenth century, 'literature' consisted of the universal writing of men, supplemented by another, separate area of feminine writing – plus a few outstanding novels written by women who were considered unrepresentative of women in general. There was little concept of female writing being of the same standard as male 'literature' – partly because male literature was seen as dealing with life, with universal themes and issues. Female literature was supposedly confined to women's issues which meant, according to Louise Bernikow, that it was regarded as 'frivolous, saccharine, decorative and inconsequential' (Bernikow, 1974, p. 21).

The recent (1980) publication of Elizabeth Robins's *The Convert* (first published in 1907 with the help of Henry James's literary agent), introduced by Jane Marcus, shows that even into the twentieth century the same principles and practices have been used against women who have crossed the established male/female literary line. If their work did not qualify for male approval but could not be prevented from being made public, then it was attacked immediately afterwards and encouraged to die a 'natural' death.

A suffragette, actress, writer and feminist, Elizabeth Robins wrote, collaboratively, the play *Votes For Women*. It was extremely successful and in the year it was first presented, it was also published in novel form as *The Convert*. Like other suffragette literature, which was largely produced by the well-organized and independent suffrage presses, *The Convert* and *Votes for Women* never became part of the mainstream literary tradition. The whole issue of the 'woman question', to which Robin's work undoubtedly contributed a great deal of real information and polemic, was never permitted to become more than an interesting and temporary phenomenon. Literary anthologies of the time, and references in history books, rarely pay more than a passing glance to the issue. With men as gatekeepers responsible for the selection of what was of genuine importance, the 'woman-question' and literary and historical commentary about it did not qualify for inclusion.

The old standby of ridicule of women when they deviated from what was considered acceptable behaviour was readily available for the critics of *Votes for Women* when it made its appearance. Marcus refers to the criticism that appeared in *The Academy* – 'Everyone was there – except the hireling critics – in the missionary spirit. The stalwart propagoose (if that be the correct feminine form for propagander) filled every available seat' (Marcus, 1980, p. ix). The implication that the play had nothing to say of universal significance, and was merely propaganda for the few converted, has been behind many of the subsequent criticisms of both the play and the novel. When such criticism, diminishing the actual subject matter of the play, is added to other comments – that the play could have been a 'very fine play' if it had not been for Robins's overcommitment to her radical and 'transitory' cause (*The Daily Mail*) – the prospects for a bright future in the literary world are not high. When the content of the play is also feminist and considered radical in its demands for women's rights, it is probably even less likely to earn male approval than Aphra Behn's poem about male impotence. Even though Robins, like Katherine Philips two centuries before, was aware of the criticism that would be thrown at her work and took the precaution of calling her play a 'tract' in order to 'defuse male critical explosions in advance' (Marcus, 1980, p. viii), *Votes For Women* as a play has had no more effect on the social reality than have votes for women in the political context.

More recently, but within the same tradition, Dorothy Richardson (1873–1957), the writer to whom the term 'stream of consciousness' was first applied (Goulianos, 1974, p. 269), has all but disappeared from literary recognition.

In my own undergraduate and graduate literary studies in Australia, which I now realize would have been better termed studies of male literature, Dorothy Richardson was not mentioned in a course on the development of the novel – a course in which the stream of consciousness technique, as exhibited by Joyce, Lawrence, Conrad and others, played a major part. I do not remember references to her work in any of the literary criticisms to which I had access in the library and certainly her very original contribution to the novel as a literary form was not acknowledged in lectures. In the light of the information now available about what is valid and what is not, her exclusion from the mainstream of literature is understandable – although by no means excusable. The first publisher to whom Richardson sent her work rejected it on the grounds that he could not understand it (Goulianos, 1974, p. 269). And why would he? In the first place, it used a technique which he had no yardstick to measure – other than the traditional expectation that women did not write as well as men. Secondly, the actual content of the book and the female consciousness that it explored would be an area quite removed from anything that he would recognize as significant. There was no precedent for a man to recognize either of these things as important – they have all been cleverly erased – and there were a great many precedents for him to presume that his judgment was 'honorable'. But because he did not recognize the significance of Richardson's work and because few others since that time have felt obliged to consider her style and concerns as anything other than 'interesting' or eccentric, there is still no precedent to regard the work of women, when it is innovative or removed from the usual concerns of the male literary system, as anything other than an exception.

Other similar examples of gatekeeping have emerged, in retrospect, in relation to the course in Australian literature which I undertook at an Australian university. I was not at the time aware that any females other than Henry Handel Richardson had written anything of note; I was certainly not aware of the rationale that may have been involved in her choosing to write under a male pseudonym. She was merely considered an eccentric. The publication in 1981 of Drusilla Modjeska's book about Australian women writers between 1925 and 1945, *Exiles at Home*, has, however, made a number of aspects of the Australian literature course presented to undergraduates in the 1960s quite clear.

By the twentieth century the literary scene in Australia, while its subject matter was becoming firmly rooted in an Australian context, was not very different from the English literary scene in terms of the place it allotted to women writers. Modjeska offers the example of Anne Brennan, a member of a literary family, and says of her Australian environment,

> There was no way for women to penetrate that bohemian
> group except through their sexuality. Women's
> intellectual and literary endeavour was simply not
> taken seriously and often, as in Anne Brennan's case, not
> even recognized. (Modjeska, 1981, p. 20)

In her observations about Anne Brennan's life, Modjeska comments,

> Here, it seems to me, is a clever, talented, intellectual
> young woman, proud of her association with a leading
> poet and the French and German intellectual and
> literary traditions in which he was an expert. She was a
> woman who had ability as a writer, who expressed her
> wish to write, and hung around the clubs where the
> writers met. Yet she did not become a writer. Instead she
> became a whore. (Modjeska, 1981, p. 20)

Unfortunately the Australian story neither begins nor ends with Anne Brennan. Earlier, in 1901, Miles Franklin's *My Brilliant Career* had been published and had proven remarkably successful in commercial terms. Franklin herself was thrown into public life and into discord with her family who were distressed at her writing and the way she had portrayed Sybilla's parents and relatives in her *fictional* work. She left Australia, as did many women writers who could find no comfortable niche in the literary and cultural world, and after 1909 published her work using pseudonyms, presumably to avoid the sorts of problems she had faced when writing under her own name. That Norman Lindsay, one of Australia's well-known literary figures, was more taken with her 'pert rump' (Modjeska, p. 35) than with the feminist

issues she explored in *My Brilliant Career* gives an indication
that the problems were not minor ones.

Another interesting Australian identity, rarely if at all
mentioned in studies of Australian literature, is Barbara
Baynton. Her first work, *Bush Studies*, was published in 1902
and was received as 'realistic beyond anything of the kind yet
written here' (*The Bulletin* quoted in Dixson, 1976, p. 77).
Several of the revered critics acknowledged her exceptional
powers but as Miriam Dixson has pointed out, with little
effect on her literary career:

> Baynton's reward for her acclaimed literary excellence
> has been something pretty close to literary oblivion. She
> threw a particularly dark light on mateship and just as
> Judith Wright's comments on this basic Australian
> male-bonding institution have been largely ignored by
> male analysts and celebrants alike of our national
> identity, so too has Baynton's illumination of it. (1976,
> p. 77)

I have just finished reading for the first time Barbara
Baynton's *Bush Studies* (they remained unpublished for over
sixty years). I was fascinated and enthralled by the stories
and angered by the commentary of A. A. Phillips which is
included in the edition as 'critical appreciation'. Phillips
refers to her stories as tending towards the 'melodramatic' (p.
30) and as 'stories of nightmare' (p. 32). He does not or cannot
allow that to women, such stories of drama and nightmare
are the genuine experiences of women's lives in a male-
dominated society and especially in the isolation and vulner-
ability that the Australian outback represents to women. His
assessment of her 'terror stories' is exemplified in his criticism of her portrayal of the viciousness of the husband in *The
Chosen Vessel*. According to Phillips, 'there was no need to
create for us the figure of the husband – his absence from the
house was all that the narration demanded of him' (p. 34). He
goes on to say, 'How vividly that passage does create him; and
how significant is the unnecessariness of the creation.'

The implication in his comment is that Baynton's sensi-
bilities are a little unbalanced – that is, not quite the same as
Phillips's. It seems to me that the portrayal of the husband is

vital to understanding the fears and emotions of the wife when she realizes another man is attempting to harass her in a far more physically threatening way. What I see as significant is not the 'unnecessariness' of Baynton's portrayal but the limitations involved in Phillips's rejection of it. His criticism denies Baynton's artistic integrity and ignores her sensibility as a female writing from a female perspective.

Phillips's disinclination to see the Australian male portrayed as a far-from-admirable creature is not unique. It was part of the literary environment when Baynton was writing and remains so today. During the 1970s in Australia a female acquaintance of mine, not known for her sympathetic attitude towards the Australian male culture, proposed an MA thesis on 'Mateship in the Australian novel'. Her proposal was rejected by the male professor on the grounds that it was not a topic! What more needs to be said?

Modjeska gives numerous other examples of the barriers erected in the face of women's literary and personal aspirations in Australia. In 1919, for example, Marjorie Barnard graduated from the University of Sydney with first-class honours in history and the university medal. She was subsequently offered a place at Oxford University but her father refused permission for her to go. She did not go. Modjeska maintains that to go without approval and support 'would have meant too big a break with her family, too much instability and insecurity' (Modjeska, 1981, p. 26). Instead, Barnard took a job as a librarian. She worked for eight hours a day, travelled for two and then played 'dutiful daughter' at home. As she herself wrote, this left her 'little time and less mental energy to write' (quoted in Modjeska, p. 76). The story is so familiar to women who write that it is absolutely astounding to hear a woman writer say that she does not have to juggle her time and her commitments in order to write. The five hundred pounds and a room of one's own that Virginia Woolf claimed was essential for women to write was no less unusual in Australia than in England and no less uncommon today than it was fifty years ago.

During the 1920s and 1930s in Australia, there was a literary upsurge, especially in the form of novels written by women. Women such as Christina Stead, Eleanor Dark,

Henry Handel Richardson, Katharine Pritchard, Dymphna Cusack, Marjorie Barnard and Flora Eldershaw (M. Barnard Eldershaw), Jean Devanny and others were producing novels and having them published. Much of the supportive environment in which they wrote was created by the rarely acknowledged networking done by Nettie Palmer who consciously and conscientiously kept in touch with many of them and provided encouragement and constructive criticism.

Nettie's husband, Vance, an aspiring writer whom she supported for much of his and her literary careers, wrote an article in 1926 entitled 'Women and the Novel', and in it demonstrated what he thought about the phenomenon of women writers. He noted, authoritatively, that the novel as a literary form was particularly suited to women and concluded that 'writing a novel seems as easy to almost any literate women as making a dress' (quoted in Modjeska, p. 8) Modjeska's comment that such was 'an extraordinarily unperceptive remark for a man who was married to a writer' (p. 8) emphasizes Palmers's inability (or reluctance) to take women and writing as seriously as he took men and writing.

Modjeska documents other examples of the prejudice and problems faced by women writers in Australia – just as they were faced by women in England and other Western countries. She draws attention to an essay written by Norman Lindsay – one of the members of the male artistic scene in Australia – in which he revealed how little he valued the contribution of women writers in Australia. Referring to the time when women were producing a great deal of commendable literature, Lindsay talked about the timidity of Australian writers and the lack of cultural leadership. In doing so he completely ignored the work of Nettie Palmer and denied the value of the work of the women writers. His literary commentary shows not just *how* women writers are excluded from acquiring validity but how easy it is for a man of letters to effect their exclusion.

The history of the development of Australian literature, when it acknowledges the contribution of the women writers, stands as a grim reminder of men's power to act as gatekeepers and arbiters of public literature. In The United States too, in fact in all the patriarchal cultures, resistance was, and is still, mounted against women writers and their work, especially when it explores new areas and new ideas that may be perceived as threatening to the established mainstream of literature. Anaïs Nin, for example, in 'The Story Of My Printing Press' published in *The Publish-It-Yourself Handbook 1980* confirms that the same situation was operating in America. When she failed to find publishers there for two of her books (one which had already been published in France and praised by Rebecca West, Henry Miller, Lawrence Durrell and others), she took the steps required to publish her own work and came across the gatekeeping system from another angle.

The difficulties that go with publishing outside the commercial presses were and are immense. Time, money and energy are all required and as Nin discovered, for the books to have any impact, reviews from the established literary critics are also essential. After Edmund Wilson favourably reviewed *Under A Glass Bell*, commercial publishers were suddenly interested in Nin's work. 'Publishers were ready to reprint both books in commercial editions' (Nin, 1980, p. 30). However, Nin found that handing over her work to the commercial press also meant that it was within their power to promote the books as they saw fit, and as they considered her an 'established writer' they saw fit not to promote her books very much. Consequently they did not reach the audience that Nin hoped to reach and her work is still read and studied by relatively few.

So it is not difficult to see how, by the late twentieth century, Tillie Olsen was able to point out that in literature courses and reading lists in the United States there is only one women writer to every twelve men and in books published, there is one woman writer for every four or five men (Olsen, 1979, p. 24), just as there was two hundred years ago (Showalter, 1978, p. 39). The guardians of literary traditions, by invoking their judgments and their penalties throughout the nineteenth century and before, have established a tradition in itself that decides that men are more creative, literary, intelligent, important and worthy of recognition than women. It is 'normal' for men to be represented in greater numbers and at higher levels in all fields of endeavour. While the list of 'lost' women writers continues to grow, it is only because of dedication by women to the recovery of their past and with tremendous cost in terms of the time and energy that could be used so productively elsewhere.

Protected from challenge, men's literary efforts have consistently been portrayed as 'better' than women's efforts and the expectation has been fostered by critics, academics and publishers that this will always be so. There is no reason to think that without radical changes, our future heritage, published or unpublished, will include women writers and thinkers in any capacity other than the one which past and present gatekeepers have devised for them.

Chapter 6

'The Race is Fair'

Contemporary Women Writers

> Literature is the 'only profession . . . which does not
> jealously exclude women from all participation in its
> honour and its profits. There is no injustice done to
> women here. The road is open. The race is fair. If woman
> be the fleeter, she wins.'
>
> (J. M. Kaye, 1857, quoted in Showalter, 1978, p. 48)

Since these sentiments were expressed during the nineteenth century, women have realized that the literary race
was and is far from fair. It was a race arranged by men and
one in which men acted as starters, linesmen, judges and
recorders of achievement. To qualify, women were obliged to
overcome handicaps that men did not face and fleetness has
proved to be of limited value in a long-range marathon. Even
when women managed to win a particular race, men's justice
has usually ensured that the 'honour and profits' they earned
were diminished in value or forgotten shortly afterwards.

But what of the race today? Ostensibly, contemporary
women are 'liberated', better educated and have greater
access than ever before to the literary world so it might be
expected that their increased contributions to our literary
heritage would be clearly visible. On the contrary, most of the
evidence points out that the handicaps and the scores in the
literary race still favour men.

Social expectations continue to work against women whenever they compete on allegedly equal terms with men. Despite the fact that well over 40 per cent of women of child-bearing age are part of the paid workforce in England, Australia, Canada and the United States, the image of woman projected in all forms of the media still emphasizes her role as proud mother, adoring wife and committed fighter of dust and dirt. Men *and* women are conditioned to see women's proper role as a private one. This means that women who take on a public role – for economic or personal reasons – face a conflict between what society expects of them and what they feel obliged to do. It is a conflict that men do not have to resolve before they can assume a comfortable existence in the public world.

Social conditioning also continues to foster the image of the male as superior. Philip Goldberg found that women expect men to be more efficient and more competent in *all* fields of endeavour, including 'traditionally feminine fields' like elementary school teaching (Goldberg, 1974, p. 40). The pervasive notion of women's inferiority or 'the big lie' as Molly Haskell calls it (quoted in Trahey, 1974, p. 61) inevitably affects women's images of themselves and requires conscious effort if it is to be overcome. 'The measureless store of belief in oneself' that Tillie Olsen mentions as essential for a writer is difficult for anyone to acquire, but as she concludes, it is 'Almost impossible for a girl, a woman' (Olsen, 1979, p. 27).

It is difficult to place contemporary writers into what will eventually emerge as the legitimate, male-approved version of literary history. As Chapters 4 and 5 have shown, the success and achievement attributed to women in their own time has often been eclipsed, through gatekeeping, within a generation. What may currently be seen as a major contribution to literature may well be 'forgotten' when the records are actually compiled.

What can be documented, however, are women's own feelings about their writing and their perceptions of the gatekeeping processes currently in operation. The revival of the feminist movement, while it may have had 'no discernible effect on book publishers in general. . . .' (Media Womens

Association, 1974, p. 134), has established a body of feminist knowledge and a network of feminist contacts to circulate it. Through feminist publications, conferences, women's studies courses, consciousness-raising groups and a myriad of women's organizations, women have gained access to each other for support, response and the sort of dialogue that in the past was only readily available to men.

Thus I have been able to communicate with a number of feminist writers, published and unpublished, in England, Australia, Canada and the United States and to record their views about writing and their experiences with the publishing industry. Through interviews, discussion and correspondence, it has been possible to make some sort of assessment of where we stand at the moment in relation to the literary world.

For obvious reasons, all the people I contacted were assured of anonymity. It was not my intention to further disadvantage women writers by naming them or the specific publishers with whom they had dealt. I also wished to have this book published without any law or libel suits. Besides, if it is true that 'anonymous was a woman' I could rationalize that anonymity would provide a familiar and comfortable persona to enable the female participants to speak out.

The responses to my enquiries revealed that women today are aware of the same limitations affecting their lives and their work as affected women writers two and three centuries ago. While the difficulties they face are not always phrased in terms of male standards and male approval, their struggles to write, to be published and to gain recognition as writers seem to depend on these criteria as surely now as they did in the past.

Before the printed word, or. . . . 'In training'
(*Notes to transcript which follow will be found on pages 125–6.*)

The following is from a letter received from an American woman writer and because it sums up much of what other women said, I have quoted it in full.[1]

Most of my experience has been in journalism of various kinds. When I first went to work . . . in New York, it was made quite clear that women could never get to be writers because the publisher believed that women could not write. So we could never aspire to be higher than researchers, which meant we supplied all the information and colour out of which writers, who never left their desks, fashioned the stories and collected twice as much pay as we did. Since 'Women's Lib' . . . things have changed technically, but in fact, there are only token women writers in the media as a whole. Whether in the US or Britain or anywhere in Europe, women do not get the interesting assignments in national or foreign affairs. I think it is not because men don't think women could do it, but because *they simply do not want to move over.* (my emphasis)

There seems little doubt that although women can now claim to be journalists and writers, men still arrange for power and authority to stay within their control. Apart from the fact that men generally receive greater financial rewards, they also receive the public recognition as writers that women are frequently denied. 'Male as writer' is a familiar concept but 'female as writer' still confounds social expectations.

A 'Women and Writing' Seminar at the Women's Research and Resources Centre in London, England in 1979 revealed that women writers, even published ones feel uncomfortable about writing for a public audience. Three writers who commented on this aspect of their writing indicate that they experience conflict when it comes to putting their thoughts on to paper.

Every time I sit down to write, I get the almost overwhelming feeling of inadequacy. Who am I to be so presumptuous? What possible evidence do I have that this is something I can expect to do?[2]
At this rate I will soon be the most quoted footnote in other peoples' articles as private correspondence. I don't seem to have any trouble writing to my friends and outlining what I'm doing. And it's not great hassle to

write papers for my study group. But I can't write for a
public audience. I simply don't seem able to send an
article to an academic journal. I don't suppose other
women have this phobia?[3]
Evidently I have to cultivate a more academic style. My
professor tells me mine is too personal. Readers will be
suspicious of me if I use the first person. That's very easy
for him to say but it is very difficult for me to do. It seems
such a posture; it sounds so insincere using the passive
voice all the time. Writing has become a most awkward
chore.[4]

Personal discussions and interviews with women in
Canada show that they experience the same sorts of doubts.
Writing is perceived as being something they cannot do
'naturally'.

It's really hard to get started – to sit at the desk and begin
to write – to WORK. I also have to make a living so
writing is either late at night or early in the morning. I
can't do it in short bursts because the quality of what you
put in is so important. . . . I mean I can't write if I'm tired
or worried about something else.[5]

Another published writer suggested that women feel
that they have to make a greater effort than their male
counterparts when presenting academic articles for publication. Her contention is that women think unless their work
is *better* than the work offered by male scholars, it does not
stand an equal chance of being accepted.[6] I have no evidence
to assume her wrong. Another writer who also works as a
housewife and mother claims,

Whenever I write I feel I am stealing time – that I should
be spending it on tasks that show some immediate
results. I can't possibly start writing until the house is
spotless, the washing is done and all household chores for
the next 24 hours are under control. It's stupid, I know,
but I guess I feel that the house and the kids are my real
responsibilities and although I need to write for the sake
of my sanity, writing has to take second place.[7]

Even when the act of writing presents few problems,

there is a tendency for women to have little faith in their material measuring up to the required 'standards'. They see rejections by publishers and agents as reflections on their ability rather than on the publishers' needs or perceived market demands.

> I sent my first manuscript to publisher after publisher.
> When it came back with recommendations, I changed it
> but it was still rejected. I thought I just didn't have what
> it takes to be a writer. Even though I have now had
> several articles and one book published, I don't feel that
> I'm a 'writer' and I still agonize over getting it 'right'.[8]

The idea that Adrienne Rich refers to of women writing for men, even when they are supposed to be addressing women (Rich, 1979, p. 38) is obviously true for a number of women already quoted. The notion that there is some standard which has to be met and that it is a standard based on the work that men have found acceptable influences women's own assessment of what is 'good' writing. Virginia Woolf drew attention in 1929 to a similar problem for women writers:

> But it is still true that before a woman can write exactly
> as she wishes to write, she has many difficulties to face.
> To begin with, there is the technical difficulty – so
> simple, apparently; in reality, so baffling – that the very
> form of the sentence does not fit her. It is a sentence made
> by men; it is too loose, too heavy, too pompous for a
> woman's use. . . . And this a woman must make for
> herself, altering and adapting the current sentence until
> she writes one that takes the natural shape of her
> thought without crushing or distorting it. (Woolf, 1979,
> p. 48)

An inveterate scribbler and in my judgment a stimulating communicator on a personal level, one particular Canadian woman explained to me about her attempts at writing:

> The one (male) person I showed my writing to informed
> me it was 'florid'. Of course it was subjective . . . it was

meant to be a record of personal experience, but florid? I haven't done any more on it since then. Maybe one day I'll pluck up courage and finish it for my grandchildren to read.[9]

It is significant that all of the women I contacted expressed some sort of doubt about their right to write and many of the comments reflect the feeling of intrusion into a man's world that Anne Finch referred to in the seventeenth century. There is often an awareness of pressure as though some sort of test has to be passed in order to qualify as a writer and it is not difficult to attribute that idea to gate-keeping based on male approval.

Women involved in publishing in Australia talked about the 'normal' gatekeeping practices that allow preferential treatment to material that reflects a male view of the world. One particular woman writer suggested that there may be a positive correlation between the acceptability of women's writing – fiction or non-fiction/feminist or masculist – and the fluctuations in Australian nationalism. During the period between 1925 and 1945, there was a huge increase in the number of women writers published, especially in fiction, and a corresponding movement of conscious nationalism (Modjeska, 1981) and it may be that a similar phenomenon is now taking place. Certainly, in Australia during the early 1980s most bookshops were visibly promoting Australiana, and perhaps under these circumstances the usual ratio of one female published author to every five males is allowed to vary. On the basis of the fate of the earlier Australian women writers, many of whom have disappeared from Australian literature with barely a trace, there is no point in antici-pating that the ratio might continue to favour women writers when publishers assess that this period of national pride is no longer a market consideration.

Transformation into print, or . . . 'Running the race'

The most obvious single piece of information to emerge from women's comments about their publishing experiences (or competing in the literary race), is that they feel their work is deemed acceptable or otherwise on the basis of its current marketability and not its message. With the exception of some women who had published with feminist presses, they also suspect publishers view this marketability as a temporary trend and in no way perceive it as a permanent shift in the demand for feminist material. Many of them referred to the 'bandwagon' that women's material, both feminist and otherwise, currently represents to publishers. Feminists were concerned about the long-term implications of this trend and felt frustrated at their inability to influence publishers' attitudes.

> The book was more or less solicited by the publisher of a small linguistics firm . . . for a series on sociolinguistics. Had it not been for the women's movement and women's studies and the hustling sense many publishers now have that there's a growing market for this sort of thing, that book and many others growing out of a feminist perspective wouldn't have been published. . . . And my sense of this is also that if the 'women's studies' market – as many publishers see it and judging from my contact with roving editors who drop round to hustle new books and authors and test out markets – starts to decline, so will the interest from mainstream publishing houses.[10]
>
> My last major publishing experience – an anthology on women which I edited – was quite easy to publish and indeed I was approached by other publishers who had heard about it and were interested. That I suppose is because women's studies is currently enjoying being on the bandwagon, which probably means it will be passé in a few years.[11]
>
> What disturbs me is . . . the realization that although many journals, even the most conservative ones, pay lip service, it makes not one scrap of difference to what they publish 'normally'. One editor of a 'learned' English journal rang me and asked me to 'ref' an article on women, making it plain that it was unlikely to be published as they had accepted one . . . a few years ago! In spite of the fact that the sociology and anthropology of women has become reasonably respectable, even

something of a bandwagon, it is still seen as a separate
topic and makes no difference to the way everything else
is taught or written about.[12]

One woman writer explained how, in 1973, while under
contract to a commercial publisher to write about women's
experience in a particular sphere, she was criticized by an
editor for covering some of the same ground that had been
covered in a book published seven years before.[13] One
wonders if the second manuscript offered to a publisher about
football was rejected because it had all been said before!

> I know that women's material is far more acceptable now
> than it was ten years ago. I was writing it then and I had
> no chance of having it accepted. The same sort of
> material is now seen as marketable. Publishers have
> approached me about doing a book to use in women's
> studies courses. I think I'll have to do it too or some man
> is going to jump on the bandwagon and write it instead –
> from *his* point of view.[14]

June Arnold in her article 'Feminist presses and feminist politics' (1976) sums up the feelings of these women
quite well when she says of the male press, 'They will publish
some of us – the least threatening, the most saleable, the
most easily controlled or a few who cannot be ignored – until
they cease publishing us because to be a woman is no longer
in style' (p. 19). Her argument has a familiar ring in terms of
the history of women's publishing experiences as we have
recovered them so far. It seems that the situation has not
changed very much.

Another experience commonly referred to by women
writers concerned marketability in another form – their own.
Lady Holland is quoted as having made dramatic pronounce-
ment during the nineteenth century that 'A name will sell
any trash' (Manley and Belcher, 1972, p. 57), and the same
principle apparently still applies. There is no question about
famous or infamous people having access to publishing if it
is thought that they themselves provide a marketable commodity. In an article about her (and recent publications have
shown her work is far from trash), a writer of fiction explained,

It was wonderful. I'd made it at twenty. But the books didn't sell well and when I offered my third – which had feminist sentiments – the publishers didn't want to know. I realized all I'd been was a saleable package – young, pretty, clever – and not out there with the rest of the student body throwing cobblestones at policemen.[15]

Another 'successful' writer commented,

I keep seeing my name bandied about as some sort of mark of approval. It does give me more exposure and I suppose publishers feel that it makes my work sell better, but I feel that my name no longer has anything to do with my thoughts or my judgment.[16]

As far as the commercial press is concerned, male approval on whatever basis they see appropriate is still the operating principle in the selection of manuscripts for publication. Feminist sentiments when they do not appear in a form suitable for use in women's studies courses or relate to a specific and popular aspect of women's experience are not gratefully received. An English writer of fiction had one feminist-oriented manuscript rejected on the grounds that it wasn't 'real literature' and another received a rejection slip with her submitted article claiming that it was 'not a topic'! Another writer in England expressed her indignation at the 'cavalier' approach of a male editor who informed her that it had never occurred to him to include a feminist contribution in the book he was editing and which was in an area she felt owed a great deal to feminism for its current developments. He dismissed her objections and claimed that he did not see the feminist material as significant.[17]

In this case the editor's right to make a judgment about what was significant depended solely on his right as a gate-keeper and not on his position as an expert in the field. Without being involved in the discipline at any level or in any capacity other than as an entrepreneur, his personal (mis)understandings were able to dictate the material to be included in a new book on the subject. The exclusion of a feminist contribution repeats the pattern of exclusion of women's material from the anthologies and edited collections that make up our published heritage.

Women writers who had worked with both commercial and feminist presses referred to a 'new breed' of feminist editors and frequently mentioned 'trust' and 'support' in their relationships with them. What some saw as advantages in dealing with a feminist editor, others saw as disadvantages inherent in negotiating on the understanding that feminism means the same thing to all women. One example centred around the writer's initially unstated assumption that there would be no editorial intervention in her article.[18]

Another felt that the particular feminist publisher she dealt with imposed even more rigid 'male' standards on her work than a male press would have done.[19] Her criticisms were met by the publisher with the claim that feminist material had to be 'better' than commercial material or it would be held up as proof of female inferiority and its credibility would be lessened. On a similar level, Barbara Gelpi, editor of *Signs: Journal of Women in Culture and Society*, says that the journal is edited more heavily than many other scholarly journals. 'We know we have to be careful in order to keep a cutting edge' (Gelpi, 1980).

Mention was made on two occasions – once by a writer and once by a feminist editor working within a commercial publishing house – of the problem that arises when feminist editors have to deal simultaneously with feminist writers and a masculist publishing establishment. The co-operation and support that are intrinsic to feminist relationships inevitably suffer at times because of the competitive pressures exerted on all editors if they wish to retain their jobs. At this stage, and as usual, it has been left to the individual feminist editors to resolve the problem of conflicting values. There is little likelihood that the commercial system will change to accommodate the inconsistencies and editors are aware that dissenters from the system are expendable. If they wish to continue to promote feminist writers and material, feminist editors have to negotiate on one level with writers and on another level with their publishing colleagues. At times the compromise may satisfy neither writer nor publisher and may satisfy the editor even less.

Generally, however, women writers who had dealt with feminist presses found them 'helpful', 'committed' and 'refreshingly open' about decision-making. I was amused by a comment from a male writing about feminist presses and who stated that while 'one' (presumably a male) could subscribe to their views and admire their dedication, one must still wonder about the 'wisdom of collective decision-making when it comes to deciding what books to publish and how they should be edited and packaged' (Wolfe, 1975, p. 4). This 'one', (definitely female), wonders in return how he thinks such decisions are made in commercial publishing if not through the collective values of men over a period of time. 'One' also wonders if he suffers from a lack of experience with co-operative values and therefore fails to understand how co-operation and consensus can work or if he, like so many other males, suffers from tunnel vision and can conceive no alternatives to established, male methods of operation.

Unlike Wolfe, many women writers were delighted by the opportunity to be involved in the publishing of their own work and were relieved to have the opportunity to present feminist material in an environment where it was valued and understood and where editing involved an expansion of rather than a limitation to their work. While there were some negative reports about experiences with feminist presses, most published writers had a tale to tell about unsatisfactory or 'alienating' experiences with the commercial presses. One example came in the form of a report about a book, co-edited by two women, one of whom was fortunate enough to see some advance publicity in a bookshop and to notice that the editors' names were given wrongly and that one of them was mis-spelt.[20] (My own copy of the same book in paperback had the cover on upside-down and back-to-front). While this is much more likely to be attributable to the binder rather than the publisher, it is part of the overall publishing process – part of 'going public' – and does not leave authors, women or men, feeling positive about their publishing experiences. In summary, it seems that while feminist writers are not always in a position to pick and choose their publishers and will often take whatever they can get, many feel that publishing with women at a feminist press promises a more rewarding personal experience then publishing with a commercial press.

I was not able to locate any women who had published with a vanity press – which process Martin J. Baron describes as being 'to legitimate publishing what loan-sharking is to banking' (Baron, 1980). 'Vanity' or 'subsidy' publishing involves paying for your work to be published, as was generally done before the appearance on the scene of commercial publishers.

Criticism of vanity publishers usually arises from their lack of commitment to selling the books that they produce. Contracts between publisher and author generally involve the author paying for publication costs plus the publisher's profits. The payment having been made, there is little incentive for the vanity publisher to expend time, money and energy selling the product. 'His' interests lie in acquiring new manuscripts rather than selling those for which he has already received payment.

In all of my reading about publishing, I have not come across a positive report on vanity publishing. This may be connected to vanity publishing being 'a species of fraud' and vanity publishers being 'hucksters' (Baron, 1980), but there may also be a connection between the negative reports and the obvious interference that vanity publishing represents in the traditional gatekeeping system. For both financial and political reasons it would be wise for those in control of commercial publishing to suppress any positive information about vanity publishing. They thus have another means of control over the market and over the material that will receive positive recognition. Criticism of vanity publishing and the material produced by this method enables the gatekeepers to keep some sort of control and to maintain their own acceptable 'standards'. It would be interesting to know if any authors, female or male, had profited either financially or personally from their association with a vanity publisher.

After the printed word, or. . . . 'Track records'

What actually happens to women's writing after it appears in print seems to depend largely on whether it is published by a big, commercial press or a smaller, alternative press. It has already been noted that material presented in paperback is less likely to be reviewed in major publications than is material published in hardcover (see p. 18). Women writers are very aware of this and their feelings about publishing with a commercial or alternative press and in paperback or cloth cover are quite ambivalent.

There is an awareness of the Catch 22 situation involved in the publication of women's material and a feeling that whichever way you choose to go, you may end up losing. Because so few women have any inside information about just how publishing decisions are made, they report feeling on unsure ground when it comes to decisions about cloth or paperback and recommended prices. From their own experience as book-buyers, they know that they will buy books that offer new feminist insights and also know that the cheaper the books are, the more likely they are to buy them immediately. However, they also seem to think that there is quite a precedent established for not recognizing cheaper editions in the forums where books are promoted and publicized. Thus, as is often the case with feminist writers, if their motivation is to reach a wide range of readers, it is difficult to know whether to agree to a cheaper edition and hope to reach people without much promotion or to push for the more expensive edition and hope that it will receive attention. The problem, it seems, is whether or not to trust the publisher's judgment when it is felt that the publisher's concerns are more with costs than with the material being published.

Women who have published with feminist presses believe there is more commitment to their work and that feminist publishers are prepared to stock and distribute it long after commercial publishers would have remaindered or shredded it. Some prefer feminist publishers for this reason and others prefer commercial publishers because of their wider distribution potential and the greater resources they have available for marketing and promotion.

One area that provoked discussion among women writers who had handed their material to the male, commercial press was the feeling of alienation they experienced once the work had gone into production. A specific example, quoted by an American writer who had been involved in compiling and editing an anthology on women, was of the discovery that the title page and the back cover of the book were devoted to the praise of the male editor of the series. As he had contributed nothing more than a letter to the total process of production, her feelings of indignation are perfectly understandable.[21] The gatekeeping process involved in this sort of appropriation of women's work is undoubtedly still with us.

Several other writers commented on the practice by commercial presses of using 'sexy' (read 'sexist') and 'suggestive' cover illustrations that in no way reflect the content of the book and which the publishers claim make it appeal to a wider audience. Women's objections centred around their exclusion from any role in deciding what is appropriate and around the trivialization of women's material implicit in this sort of representation. Again it was mentioned on several occasions that commercial presses rarely had a genuine sense of commitment to women's material.

Reception by the critics, which continues to play a large part in determining the fate of any published work, also provoked a great deal of response from women writers. When not ignored,* the old standby of ridiculing women's work precisely because it is different from men's work and on the assumption that men have 'got it right' is seen as a major problem and one which most women feel they can do little to counteract. Feminist writing, when it is subversive or deals with new concepts and understandings, has been trivialized since Mary Wollstonecraft's *A Vindication of the Rights of Woman* in 1792, and contemporary writers know that trivialization is a gatekeeping technique that is still readily available for use. Reviews in the commercial press of current feminist material frequently attempt to diminish its significance by alluding to the 'man-hating' qualities and the 'humourlessness' of the authors.[22] As with Mary Wollstonecraft, the ideas are either not addressed or are treated

---

* Currently, Dale Spender and Amanda Spry are doing research on the presence of women's work in the review sections of major English newspapers: their preliminary findings are astonishing. The average space allocated to women's writing in the papers so far checked is 6 per cent.

patronizingly as minor, even if perspicacious, departures from 'real', masculist material. It will be interesting to see, at the end of this decade, just how many feminist contributions to our culture have been adopted into the mainstream of publicly available 'knowledge'. It will be even more interesting to determine how many of them have been attributed openly to feminists and feminist scholarship.

Overview

The concept of the 'literary race' as a fair one is a concept that only men could believe. For them, there may be a rational connection between what they *are*, what they *do* and the judgment and prizes that are awarded to them. But for women the race is 'fixed'. There is no sensible connection between our performance and the judges' decisions. As the second sex (de Beauvoir, 1972), women are obliged to come from behind merely to qualify for the race. We then risk disqualification at any stage before, during or after it on any grounds that the male judges care to name. It is quite acceptable for men to impose limitations on women's access to training for the race and then to criticize our performance as less professional than that of our more experienced and better-conditioned male counterparts.

What emerges quite clearly is that if women wish to run in the race, then the appropriate context is in competition with each other at minor and alternative track meets and with an audience of female spectators. Meanwhile men, with more sponsors, better funding and a universal audience, can organize and participate in the 'Olympics' where they can be assured of greater prizes, not the least of which is justification for their continued supremacy. They may allow an occasional 'benefit' to satisfy public demand for female performers but everyone should be aware that the *real* race is a man's race. Women should not be allowed to compete in it and must certainly not be allowed to be recorded as the winners!

Chapter 7

An Obstacle Race

Women in Publishing

I knew that in 1974 the Media Women's Association had declared that women in publishing generally held what they considered to be the equivalent to the 'janitor's job – if they had the right looks, the right credentials, and an ability to type. And knew someone' (Strainchamps, 1974, p. 133). What I wanted to find out in the early 1980s was whether women still occupied low positions with minimal input into decision-making, and if so, what gatekeeping techniques were being used to arrange the obstacles in women's way.

My initial attempts to penetrate the publishing mystique were not notable for their success. I contacted editorial representatives from a variety of different publishing houses in all four countries (Canada, USA, Australia, England) and made a point of approaching as many men as women in my initial requests for interviews and discussions. I felt this was being 'honourable' in the established tradition.

My first contact was with a male editor and was a response to a formal, written request for an interview about 'the role of women in publishing'. I was informed by telephone and rather patronizingly, that the gentleman was 'not concerned with women's issues – only human ones'.[23]

While still recovering from the imputation of my non-human status, my second contact came in the form of a written reply in response to a similar request of a managing editor. It was a standard rejection slip stating that his company was not accepting any unsolicited manuscripts at that time. As my request for an interview could not be interpreted as a manuscript, I gather that my letter was not read.[24]

Undaunted, I tried farther afield and became engaged in a telephone conversation with an editorial assistant who explained that publishers did not like talking about their 'standards' to outsiders. I was not able to ascertain any reason for this other than 'they can't really afford to divulge that sort of information'.[25]

At this early stage, I had a presentiment that acquiring any 'inside' information was not going to be easy. Short of my infiltrating the system as an undercover spy, I could see no approach that would provide me with the information that I was seeking. However, I did eventually manage to interview fourteen publishing representatives from four different countries and to discuss the subject on a number of occasions with writers, editors and reviewers in formal and informal situations. Although the same number of women and men were initially approached, I had more, positive responses from females, and probably appropriately accumulated more information from them. Five males and nine females, four of whom were feminists, supplied information about their roles and their perceptions of women's current positions in the publishing world.

I also submitted an unsolicited proposal, based on this book, to twelve publishers and recorded their responses. Of the twelve, only eight had replied within six months of my sending the proposal. Three replies, the earliest responses, were from the three feminist publishers approached. Two of these rejected the proposal on the grounds that it was not the type of book they published but both recommended other feminist publishers who might be interested. The third sent a standard reply form explaining that all manuscripts are initially considered by two people and that if interest is shown, further decision-making is a collective process and quite a 'lengthy' one. The letter mentioned three or four months: one year later nothing further has been heard.

The five replies received from commercial publishers (all

of whom were chosen as likely prospects from the 46th edition of *Writers' Market*) were all rejections. Three were in the form of standard rejection slips indicating that the proposal did not suit their present needs. One was a personal note and the other an extremely polite explanation stating that 'after much careful thought we have rather reluctantly concluded that it will be a little too specialized for inclusion in our list at the present time' and that 'this decision is based on ... commercial assessment of the potential market and should not be interpreted as masculine prejudice against the subject matter of the book'.[26] It was signed by the editorial director and also contained recommendations for other, more likely outlets. With a score of none out of twelve, it seemed that reports of the difficulties faced by unknown writers in their attempts to break into print had not been exaggerated.

The questions that I asked in interviews were centred around three main areas: (1) Who held which jobs in publishing and why; (2) On what bases manuscripts and writers were selected and who was involved in the decision-making processes; (3) How feminists working in publishing viewed the whole publishing industry and their particular role within it. With each of the people interviewed I raised the issue of gatekeeping at some stage.

Who hold which jobs and why?

Traditional stereotypes are alive and well within the publishing industry. Although exceptions exist, men are the 'doers' – the *public* agents who initiate the action, receive the feedback and are thus in positions to instigate the processes involved in naming issues of concern. Women take on the *private* roles within the companies and fill most of the desk jobs, especially if there is any typing involved.

Each of the editors, male and female, was asked if they thought women were discriminated against within the industry generally and if they considered their own company favoured men for some positions and women for others. Their answers stand as evidence of the 'arrangements' that continue to place women and men into traditional, stereotyped roles.

I don't know about publishing generally but I am not aware of any discrimination here. Most of the women who work inside are there because they want to be not because they have to be. They could be more ambitious. I do know that I discriminate in favour of women when it comes to looking for writers in my area [literature and humanities]. I suspect that it is balanced out by men writers being viewed more favourably in areas relating to science or technology. But I couldn't say for sure.[27]

The editor involved in this interview was quite unaware of the stereotyping involved in associating women with literature and humanities and men with science and technology. Last century, of course, women could not *do* literature and humanities because they were not exposed to these subjects in any depth in their education. Now, when science and technology are considered more valuable in a pragmatic sense, women are not seen as competent in these areas. There was no analysis of *why* women might want to be 'inside' rather than 'outside', just an acceptance that this was so.

There's no discrimination here, although I have to admit that there aren't many women right at the top of publishing in this country [Canada]. But here, whoever does the best job, gets the job. Usually women don't want the jobs that require follow-up work, after hours; they're more involved with family and personal ties than the men are. We have one woman editor who is single and she does the same job as the men – and just as well too – maybe even better.[28]

The speaker quoted here apparently saw nothing contradictory in the opening comment presumably because it is normal for there to be few women 'right at the top of publishing'. He assumed that the women he worked with operated on the same bases as men but 'chose' differently. There is no understanding that women's 'family and personal ties' might represent an essential caretaking role – a responsibility from which many working men are frequently absolved. There is also the rather irritating assumption in his comments that the way men *do* certain jobs is the *right* way. Under these circumstances non-discrimination means allowing women to do the men's jobs the way that men do them.

> The only area I can see where women aren't really equal
> is travelling. There is only one [woman] in sales here.
> They used not be allowed to do the travelling because of
> the trouble they would have carting heavy books around
> and it means being away for long periods of time
>
> *(Question: What about men being away for long periods of time?)*
>
> I suppose that's just accepted as normal. Like women
> doing the typing. We have some men who can do their
> own, but they'd rather not.[29]

What is being referred to as 'normal' is society's approval of the male prerogative to move freely in the world and society's expectation that women stay confined within a particular space, performing the tasks that men do not like to do. The limitations imposed on women through the pressure of conforming to social expectations are also demonstrated in the following comment where the female editor seems unaware that she is not really accepted as rightful heir to a 'male' position. She does not doubt that men are the best judges of a 'good' idea and operates on the basis of male approval, just as women writers are obliged to do.

> There's no overt discrimination here. If there was,
> I wouldn't have my job. It's more a feeling. There are
> times at meetings when I get the impression that some
> of the men, mainly the older ones, wish I'd just be quiet
> so they can get on with the job. It's never stated but
> I think they feel I should be home doing the cooking or
> out having a good time like their daughters. But, if
> I have a good idea, they'll listen and help with the
> follow-up.[30]

From this interview it seemed apparent that in this company, the appointment of a woman editor was both a token gesture towards women's equality, (the managing editor informed me that they had *women* working at all levels), and a way to brighten up the office. It also seemed to me that a subtle form of harassment was being practised on the female editor through the paternal attitudes expressed towards her. There is a way in which the 'follow-up' help with her good ideas managed to make use of her insights and abilities without acknowledging their, or her, contribution.

> I'm here because we recently started to take women's issues a bit more seriously and I got promoted to deal with it. I don't push the feminist bit too far. Everyone here knows I'm a feminist but I encourage them to think it doesn't affect my work. Anything that relates specifically to women comes to me. It's my special interest and they assume I'm working from the same premises as they, but I just know more about it . . . My boss sometimes vetoes my ideas and it's seen as quite OK for anyone to comment about my area, but I'm never approached to contribute anything to the other sections. I suppose when it comes to promotion, I'll be too specialized to move into a line position. For the moment though, I'm happy being accommodating on the surface and subversive underneath it all.[31]

Again the woman editor is valued only when her work meets with male approval and while it remains within a clearly defined area. This is also an example of a woman being pressured into pretending conformity to male values in order to work within a male system. There is no idea of her having any access to power or any input into decision-making. The role of decision-maker, even on women's issues, is a male role.

> I am regarded as very much a junior and I'm not in a position to make much of the feminist angle. Whenever I've given any sort of feminist analysis, its been 'edited' without any explanation to me. I have been warned that we are supposed to be catering for *all* women, but no one has ever mentioned why specifically feminist stuff can't be printed. I haven't given up yet, but I wonder if other people get to the stage where they just leave

it out in the first place . . . it would be a whole lot easier.[32]

It is possible for publishers to play the equal numbers game and give the impression that they are making more positions available to women when, as in this case, they can be assured that the individual woman (and women generally) receive no genuine support for a female perspective. Consistent censure and failure to meet with approval from the upper levels might even work to co-opt the appointed woman into adopting the approved male point of view. What a coup!

Whilst few of the people interviewed were aware of explicit examples of overt personal discrimination by anyone, against anyone, some women who had recently been promoted to positions which had previously denoted a certain level of authority felt their positions were little more than tokens. Although they had the opportunity to sit in on decision-making meetings, they felt the actual dialogue which led up to the decisions had taken place elsewhere and without their input. As one woman explained, 'If you haven't got any particular clout in the company – like owning it – then it's wise not to aim too high!'[33]

I am now allowed to attend board meetings every Tuesday but what I say there never counts for much – unless it's in an area where I have a contact and they don't. I get the impression that the decisions are more than half made before the meetings even take place. It's not unusual for a topic to be introduced by one of the male editors through reference to a conversation he's had with some of the others over lunch or the night before. I don't lunch with them and I don't meet with them after work. I'm not usually invited and when I am, I don't get much of a chance to say anything. Really, most of the time, I may as well be sitting at my desk as a secretary. At least I felt competent there.[34]

The perennial problem of women's lack of expertise in certain areas (from which they have been excluded) being used to deny them positions seems to be as prevalent now as it was in the eighteenth century when women were objecting to their enforced lack of education being used to deny them access to a public role. It is obviously not difficult for men who have never been confronted with women in any role other than those which men have arranged for them, to imagine that women have no desire to move out of those prescribed roles. It is not difficult to provide a defence in terms of 'it didn't occur to me' or 'I had no idea'. As most men have made very little effort to read any of the literature that women have written dealing with just this problem, they can continue to feel vindicated in assuming that women only work to fill in time and for what only men could have termed 'pin-money'.

> Most of us [women] – and there aren't that many of us – know that the men have suspicions that we are not quite as serious about our work as they are. Just the comments about weekend activities are enough to let you know that they think we're all just filling in time until the knight in shining armour comes along. Then there's the added problem that a lot of women don't have the opportunity to find out much about the business side of publishing. I've always been given what amounts to piece-work and had to be quite troublesome to be allowed into the commercial side as well. I don't know whether the resistance was due to a conscious awareness of my becoming a 'competitor' or something less sinister but the general impression that women don't belong on the managerial side, and that I was being aggressive and assertive in wanting to get more experience, is fairly common.[35]

Several women also mentioned that there were very few of their male colleagues whom they felt regarded them as professional equals. It may be that women are still relatively new in the area or that men generally have not yet come to terms with the fact that they are likely to find women involved in areas of public life that were previously reserved for men, but either way, many men still apparently find it distracting to confront a woman in a professional business arrangement.

It's a minor detail really but manages very effectively to put you in your place. You know how men when they meet each other all shake hands and immediately include each other as like-minded people? Well, I'm continually in the position of being politely acknowledged while the men shake hands – even though my official title is the same as theirs. I'm immediately put into a different category and that does affect me and the discussions we're involved in.[36]

The men I approached about this sort of behaviour explained it in terms of social custom rather than any form of discrimination. They were not 'used to' women shaking hands and therefore either forgot to do so or were embarrassed and avoided doing so. I asked one particular man who was obviously taken aback by my outstretched hand how he thought he would react to a man who rejected a handshake. It was meant as a fairly serious question but not taken as such. 'I don't meet many men who look like you' was the answer. There didn't seem much point in pursuing the conversation further.

Questions about discrimination also brought out an element of hostility from some of the men towards what they saw as unfair privileges being granted to women. There were several references to the guidelines for fair publishing brought out by the McGraw-Hill Book Company and the Macmillan Publishing Company and to the notion that women were getting more help and were being given more allowances than their male counterparts.

If there is any discrimination here it is for women and not against them. We [presumably men] have to be constantly aware that we're not upsetting some woman and I can assure you that they don't worry about upsetting us. Not that there's really any antagonism but some of us have been disturbed by one woman in particular who keeps quoting from the Macmillan guidelines and warning us that our ideas are sexist. It's not a very effective way to get things done. Five years ago there weren't any women in positions to say that sort of thing, let alone a set of written guidelines to quote from.[37]

I am indebted to Dale Spender for her analysis of a similar situation in regard to men, women and language. She points out that the male-determined social reality requires that women be silent and 'when women are supposed to be quiet, a talkative one is one who talks at all' (Spender 1980b, p. 43). In the same way, it seems highly probable that what men in publishing were objecting to was not that women are now being given a few minor positions in the publishing hierarchy or even that editors were being asked to be aware of a few major examples of sexist practices in their decision-making roles. What disturbed them was that they had to consider women in any role at all in an area that has traditionally been seen as a 'man's world', where the prerogatives have been men's to do with as they pleased. Under these circumstances any interference by women as agents acting on their behalf can be interpreted as unfair.

Selection of writers and manuscripts

All editors and publishers agreed that 'networks' or established systems of contact were fundamental to the processes of finding manuscripts, developing ideas and material and locating writers for particular projects. It did not surprise any of them that a contract for a book could be awarded entirely on the basis of recommendations within the network and without anyone having met the writer or having read any of his or her work.

I asked each of the publishing representatives how they actually 'discovered' manuscripts and located writers. None of them had dealt with more than two unsolicited manuscripts in the past twelve months. Instead, most of the work that had reached the stage of being considered for publication came from published writers who already belonged to the publishing company's own 'stable' or were commissioned by editors, from writers who were already known, at least by reputation. Reference was made to a sort of honour system that prevented editors from stealing writers from other companies but, like all honour systems, there were named instances of the honour being broken.

> Mostly it's contacts and knowing who is doing what in what area. We signed a contract once with a writer that no one here had met and no one had read her work. It was all done through recommendations. She is in the States and it was a matter of getting her to sign before anyone else could. We had such good reports about what she was doing that we negotiated the contract sight unseen. It is working out well but I know there have been others which have been awful failures.[38]

> Generally it's a matter of favours within the industry. You know, you'll be aware someone is looking for a publisher in a certain field and then you talk to an editor who is interested in the same topic or the same point of view and you provide the connection. It always comes back sooner or later. The editor will let you know about it when he hears of something that might be useful. Our travellers provide us with a lot of information. They talk to librarians and teachers and find out where there's a need for new books and we find someone to do them. Somebody always seems to know somebody who is researching the area or already writing about it. Editors have remarkable networks. That's what their job is about.[39]

Undoubtedly, there is a circle of people who know each other and who are prepared to provide connections on the understanding that the favour is reciprocated. This serves to keep the publishing networks operating on a closed-shop basis. Outsiders are not usually welcomed nor is any material which might disturb an otherwise very manageable system.

> We are always looking for writers or projects we think will be popular. Mostly we stick to people who have an established reputation – we contact them or they contact us. More often nowadays, an agent will come up with something that seems likely. They have a fair idea of what we want and if we know them and their standards

we'll listen to what they have to say. We can't afford to
take on new authors or new ideas where there isn't an
established market. Frankly, we just don't have that sort
of money.[40]

All of the people in publishing were very conscious of the
'money' or the commercial aspects of their role. There were
frequent references to 'rising costs' and the limitations they
imposed on publications – both in range and in number. The
only answer that I could elicit as to what finally swayed the
balance and allowed one manuscript rather than another to
meet with approval by all the parties concerned came from a
female editor.

It sounds silly but the go-ahead can be based on one
person's enthusiasm. We had a book written by an
'intimate' friend of one of the senior editors. Several
people had looked at it and no one was really sure
whether it was top-rating but he seemed so sure and he
doesn't usually make mistakes. So it went through.[41]

I asked if it had sold very well. The answer was a chuckle and
a 'no'.

I'm not a feminist but I do establish women as contacts
and use them when I can. It's the only way I can compete
with the men by having some contacts that they don't
have. I suppose you could call that an old girls' network.
It doesn't sound quite as glamorous as the old boys, does
it? I mean – old girls? I just see it as a way of evening
things up a bit.[42]
    It's not a conscious move to keep men out just as I
don't think they deliberately plan to exclude me. It just
seems natural that the people I contact and get on well
with are women. I meet them at seminars and everything
and we swap views and information. The men do it, I
know, and they don't see it as unfair. So we do it too.[43]

Non-feminist women in publishing resisted a conspiracy
theory that implicated men in women's exclusion from male
networks and from the top positions. Although they admitted
that male networks served to keep women out of many of the

important projects, they were reluctant to see the arrangements as deliberate or political. Feminist women who *do* see their networks as having a specifically political function take it for granted that male networks perform the same function.

'Networks' also include the referees and reviewers who are called upon by editors to give their unbiased and informed opinions about the content, style and marketability of proposed material. I asked how referees and reviewers were chosen. Some publishing companies apparently pay a small sum to specific people within a certain area to act as advisors. Others approach the 'experts' in whatever field the manuscript deals. There was considerable difference of opinion about the effectiveness of this method as a genuine guide to the potential of the material.

> Our refs are all academic people. They have busy schedules but I know several of them well enough to get a quick response if it is essential. You can't insist on receiving the report within a week but generally if we allow them enough time, they are very responsive. We have published some of them before in other publications.[44]
> ... [the managing editor] usually recommends the people who are likely to be the best reviewers. He knows a lot of them personally. We have gone ahead and published when the reports have been negative but mostly we decide along the lines that reviewers recommend ... the marketing people make a fuss otherwise.[45]

One feminist editor saw the referee system as 'red-tape' which may have served a rational purpose at some stage but which now serves as a cover to hide the personal and political choices made by publishers and editors.

> Do you know, I suggested as a joke that I would send an article to my friends for reports. No one laughed. Of course you send particular manuscripts to particular referees on the basis of whether or not you want to publish them. You know who will like them and who won't. You arrange for two positives if you like the

article and for two negatives if you don't. In the final
analysis you make the decision yourself but you drum up
some support before you make a public presentation.[46]

Perhaps the most significant single contribution about
women in publishing came from a feminist in England who
has worked with both feminist and commercial presses. The
analysis of her own publishing experiences provides a focus
for many of the other comments.

When I think of my introduction to editing, I almost
want to disappear with embarrassment at my own
naïvety. I honestly believed I would be a neutral cog in
the process – that articles would be forwarded to me –
that I would send them out to reviewers for objective
criticism and that I would have a basis for accepting or
rejecting certain articles. Apart from the fact that
choosing reviewers is not an objective process, that the
reviewers do not write objective criticism and that
decisions of whether or not to publish are most
subjective, there is the fact that I completely overlooked
the process of the commissioned or the 'invited' article.
    Now I look at the body of work that I have helped
'initiate' and I can see the enormous interventions that I
have been engaged in. And I am not always comfortable
about that. That is why I am offering this information.
Books like this need to be written.
    My first 'intervention' came after a meeting one day,
where a group of women (low on the hierarchy) were
trying to convince a group of men (high on the hierarchy)
that the laws pertaining to sex equality were not
working. They were quoting cases which were just, but
which had been lost; cases which had not been taken up
and cases where the burden an individual woman was
asked to bear, in order to challenge employers, was too
great in emotional or financial terms. The men were
convinced that the women had received more than
their share of the cake since legislation for equal
opportunity and not only did they dismiss the women's
experience, they challenged the source of their evidence.
I can remember one distinguished man saying he had

never seen a single article which would support the
women's views and I decided there and then that he soon
would!

I did a lot of telephoning that night and
commissioned three pieces of work documenting the
inadequacies of equality legislation and the fact that it
had changed nothing. Although not all of it came to
fruition, some of it did.

It was really only after I had done it that I
appreciated the significance of my action. I had been
instrumental in creating new 'truths' for my own
political purposes. I wasn't terribly distressed about my
action. What hit me was how easy it was and that if I
could do this, so could a lot of other people. To me this was
an incredible insight into the way publishers and editors
can create 'truths' and as a feminist and knowing that
most of those publishers and editors are men, I realized
how easily and how often they must influence the course
of discussion and debate over a wide sphere.[47]

It seemed to me that this was evidence of the sort of
gatekeeping that has always been practised in publishing
but which has been seen as 'normal' and 'honourable' by the
men who have been convinced that their world view is the
right view. I have no doubt that these comments will be seen
as evidence of 'dishonourable' practice but the only difference
between this example of intervention and those documented
in Chapters 4 and 5 is that this intervention has been consciously practised and its political nature explicitly acknowledged. None of the information acquired from any of the
sources I contacted in the publishing industry led me to alter
my thesis that publishing does not take place on a rational
basis and that a system of unacknowledged male gatekeeping provides much of the irrationality.

Women in feminist publishing

The major issue emerging from discussion and interviews
with women involved in feminist publishing was the distinct
awareness that their selection of material and writers as well

as their choice of contacts has a political dimension. The name 'feminist' is a declaration of interest in women and of open commitment to women's concerns.

> You would think being labelled feminist and concerned with 52 per cent of the population would ensure success for feminist publishers. But it often works the other way. A lot of people still dismiss feminist publications as minor or radical before they even read them. We've had people surprised to find that our children's books are 'really good' after they've seen them associated with a feminist press in a review. Regardless of what it's about, people just dismiss it. I sometimes wonder if they think they'll find a burnt bra inside.[48]
>
> We have networks, as you call them, but not to discover new issues. We are quite familiar, as feminists, with the important issues for women. Our referees are chosen because of their familiarity with the field of work and it is the content that we want refereed – we already know what we think of the political aspect of the work. It has to be feminist or we wouldn't consider it for publication.[49]

A feminist editor in the United States drew attention to the fact that a similar bias – but towards men – operates in mainstream publishing but it is not acknowledged as political.

> Men have done the same thing for years but on the pretence that their work was objective. Who ever heard of masculist literature? Or a masculist press? But that's what it is. Men's literature is considered *real* literature and everything else is an imitiation and not the real thing.[50]

Involved with the political dimension of feminist publishing was a sense of commitment to a cause. Feminist publishing is not *primarily* a money-making concern; it is a political concern with cultural and personal dimensions. The shared commitment and the co-operative nature of the processes produce rewards that were not mentioned by the people involved in other publishing organizations. The women in feminist publishing were convinced of the value of their material and of their contributions to building and spreading feminist information and understandings.

> It's something that has to be done. In a way I see it as my contribution – giving back some of what has been given to me. I'd like it to be more profitable – of course – but it's a different world from the big hard world out there. I really get something out of this that I never got on the commercial cocktail scene.[51]

The justification for feminist publishing is political. The people involved in its production know that the material they promote is subversive and threatening to the male-dominated society. Some of them have had break-ins and property damage and do not pretend that such events have been arbitrary. Efforts to limit the influence and the place of feminist publishing in our society cannot be seen as motivated merely by commmercial competition.

The second issue that came up in each of the discussions about feminist publishing dealt with the perennial lack of funds that feminist publishers face. It was pointed out that according to the United Nations 'State of the World's Women' Report (1980), women own only 1 per cent of the world's wealth and this is 'not enough to go around'.[52] Almost without exception, feminist publishers are battling with financial problems. Whether they are publishing books, periodicals or newspapers, they tend to operate on voluntary or poorly paid labour and to put in exceptionally long hours (Wolfe, 1980). 'Only by virtue of immense amounts of donated time and energy (from writers as well as publishers) . . . is feminist publishing alive today. (Grimstad, 1979, p. 105).

The lack of resources brings with it a number of problems. It means that feminist presses cannot compete with the big commercial houses in terms of advertising or promotion and 'we can't offer the same broad distribution and advances to authors' (Grimstad, 1979, p. 107) It also means a lack of influence and political clout. Naming an issue within a feminist context does not necessarily mean that the issue will receive recognition outside or inside feminist circles. There is even the possibility that naming an issue in a feminist publication can preclude its circulation to a wider audience. June Arnold maintains that women's presses and journals are deliberately excluded from reviews in *Publishers' Weekly*, the *New York Times* and the *Village Voice* in the United States because they know 'we are engaged in the essential struggle to develop our politics, strengthen our voices and make certain our movement prevails' (Arnold, 1976, p. 125). In other words, feminist presses are the object of deliberate gatekeeping on the part of the established and threatened commercial presses, who have most to lose from their increased acceptability. For the women involved in feminist publishing, this inevitably adds a political dimension to their work.

Also identified with their lack of resources is the problem that feminists see associated with their circulation being limited to white, middle-class women while immigrant and working-class women, often the most exploited, are not exposed to the information (Wolfe, 1980). Feminist material is not readily available in local stores. That space has been commandeered by commercial publishers and filled with 'pulp and pop' (West, 1978, p. 7).

> The revival of interest in women's material has provided a fairly solid financial base for some of us. Reprints of old books, especially if the copyright has run out, have given feminist presses enough to push new material and, hopefully, to distribute it more widely than we have been able to before. But there is a sense in which we can't promote ideas the way they [commercial presses] do. Our budget doesn't permit it and we try to keep costs down so that our books aren't expensive. I alternate between being madly optimistic and feeling depressed that we'll never really have it read by any more than the already converted.[53]

Overview

The information provided by people in publishing indicates that gatekeeping controls still work, directly and indirectly, to prevent women from acquiring power or authority within the industry. Decision-making positions are no more readily available now than they were ten or a hundred years ago and feminist presses are restricted to the role that the commercial publishing establishment allows for them.

In non-feminist organizations women's roles are dictated by men's needs and are valued according to men's expectations. Because men are accustomed to regarding themselves as central, and to interpreting evidence in their own favour, they are prone to assume that women's decisions are as autonomous as their own. They seem to have no overt awareness that women are not equal; they do not see that women may operate from premises which are quite different from men's. It is not difficult for them to argue that it is 1980 and 'all's well' when they are using their own experience as the basis for judgment, for it is fundamental to the whole problem for women that men neither know nor consider *our* experience. Nor are they likely to while the system as it presently operates excludes women from the after-hours meetings and the all-male networks and at the same time allows men to rationalize that women have *chosen* their exclusion. There is no concept that the system should change to accommodate women's different needs and values; there is no acknowledgment that it provides a series of advantages for men. Either men do not have the ability to see beyond their desks, which I doubt, or they refuse to see beyond their desks if it means that they may have to share them with women. I suspect that the latter explanation comes closer to the truth.

Feminist material is regarded by commercial publishers as a 'topic' – one with a beginning and an end. As soon as it belongs to the male-controlled system it can be printed, promoted or allowed to go out of print as the publishers see fit. While it offers financial rewards it may be tolerated as it has been at times in the past, but there is little indication of any commitment to feminist work as genuine knowledge. Information and ideas about men are not seen as part of a topic but as representative of life and having universal appeal and value. The notion that material relating to men and men's interests might have a beginning and an end is ludicrous.

Within feminist organizations, women do have personal autonomy. They can make decisions on the basis of their own understandings and their own values, frequently operating collectively. But in a political or power context, male dominance in the society at large dictates that women's contributions will have less authority and less validity than society automatically grants to men and their output. The resources and the influence that have accrued to male-controlled publishing organizations allow men to determine the market conditions and the acceptability of *all* published material. Gatekeeping practices that have served to project the image of feminists as radical, anti-male and anti-society have pushed feminist publishers and publications into a marginal position and for both financial and political reasons, it suits men for them to stay there.

Chapter 8

Power and Print

It is no longer possible to ignore the connection between women's absence from our published heritage and male control of the printed word. For centuries the male-dominated publishing industry has decided what will be presented in print and has determined its form, content and status. The consistency with which those in the industry have employed the same techniques of control during that time indicates the operation of a systematic and purposeful series of 'arrangements' (Millett, 1971, p. 23) to limit the impact of women's work in print.

Louise Bernikow says that 'most women writers have gotten lost' (1974, p. 4) and in each case, *someone has lost them*. Information in this book indicates that the someone has usually been a member of the dominant male group and that it has been in his interests to make it difficult for women to create and circulate their own knowledge. It has suited him to prevent women's truths from earning a significant place in our literary history and from acquiring the validity and authority granted to his truths.

Under these circumstances, statements referring to women's writing as 'in print' or 'out of print' become political statements. They relate directly to men's *power* over women's words and denote active intervention by men in the processes whereby women's knowledge acquires significance and legitimacy.

And it is towards the exercise of power over their words and their lives that women's struggle for autonomy and for recognition of their ideas in print has been directed. Each woman writer who has explored or exposed the mythical nature of male supremacy and the injustices of the system that it supports has actually been attacking the established power structures. Each gatekeeping technique brought out to put her in her 'proper' place has been an effort to diminish the effectiveness of her attack and to retain power and authority within male control.

In 1869 John Stuart Mill declared that those whose power was based on 'might is right' (as men's undoubtedly is) had never given an inch until 'physical power had passed to the other side' (quoted in McWilliams-Tullberg, 1977, p. 144). Both women's and men's knowledge support his view and it is worth considering the information currently available on publishing and the printed word in the light of his 'truth'.

Physical power has not yet passed to 'the other side', nor is there any evidence that men intend to relinquish their power out of a sense of justice or commitment to women's equality. If that were the case, the United States would have ratified the Equal Rights Amendment, England's Equal Opportunity legislation would be working to improve women's conditions, the men currently responsible for shaping Canada's constitution would automatically have included equal rights as a fundamental principle, and Australia would not be a 'man's country'. None of these things has happened. The concessions granted to women have only come when pressure has been applied. Gains have been made on the rare occasions when women have been able to use the male system to work against men, or when men have been assured that they can cease one gatekeeping practice because others are operating with equal effectiveness! It is possible, then, that what we have perceived as gains in the movement towards equality are themselves manifestations of gatekeeping. It is probable that the increased popularity of feminist material, the appointment of more feminists into positions in commercial publishing and the apparent growth of feminist publishing, while they are of tremendous value to women and the women's movement, are really manoeuvres to block rather than facilitate fundamental changes in the distribution of power.

Frequently in the past, what women have assumed to be significant, long-term gains in their status have proven to be temporary concessions and have been subsequently withdrawn. For example, when Mrs Oliphant declared the nineteenth century to be 'the age of female novelists' (quoted in Showalter, 1978, p. 75), it would not have been surprising if others had considered that women's creative and literary ability had been established once and for all. It must have seemed to them that literature from that time would reflect considerable changes in the attitudes towards women writers and that literary history would include them in far greater numbers than ever before.

But this has not been the case. Instead we have the phenomenon of 'residual Great Traditionalism' whereby 'the concept of greatness for women novelists often turns out to mean four or five writers . . . and even theoretical studies of "the woman novelist" turn out to be endless recyclings and recombinations of insights about "indispensable Jane and George" ' (Showalter, 1978, p. 7). Acceptance of a few women writers by the literary establishment has served marvellously well for the rejection of many, many others, and this goes a long way towards explaining why the literary gatekeepers have allowed any female writers at all to occupy major positions within the literary tradition.

Richard Altick put the proportion of published books by women in relation to men between 1800 and 1935 fairly consistently at 20 per cent (quoted in Showalter, 1978, p. 39), and today Tillie Olsen suggests that 'four to five books are published by men to every one by a woman' (Olsen, 1979, p. 24). Apparently there has been little change in the general consensus among men who select material for publication. Providing female contributions are contained at an agreed and manageable level, they are allowed to exist. So while women may have discovered their power to write, men's power over what they write has ensured that male supremacy in literature, as elsewhere, has not been seriously threatened. The concept of 'man' as the genuinely creative person has remained unchallenged.

In other cases, too, what have been taken by women as genuine advances in their struggle for autonomy have eventually emerged as little more than token gestures to deflect criticism from men or to gain time while the centres of power have been moved to other less accessible areas.

When women were finally 'granted' the right to vote, it seemed they had at last gained some say in determining their own lives. But this was far from what actually happened. In England, for example, those who originally held the right to vote were the wealthy gentry who did play some part in deciding policy and therefore wielded some power.

However, by the time women were permitted to vote, the relationship between power and suffrage had been almost totally eroded. The power associated with decision-making remained in the hands of wealthy and influential men and what women were awarded was the luxury of massaging men's egos by endorsing one male point of view rather than another. Far from heralding a new era of justice for women, the vote signified a shift in power away from women (who no longer had a visible cause to fight for) and entrenched it more firmly in the hands of those men already in positions of wealth and power. It gave few benefits of substance to women and demanded no sacrifices on the part of men. It certainly did not alter the established female/male balance of power.

There was not then and there is not now much real connection between women's ideals and those of their political representatives. Even when women themselves have been elected to office, the system works so that their tenure depends more on their advocacy of male values than on presentation of their own. Besides, according to a study done in Canada in 1979, in that country at least, it will take another 842 years before women gain equal representation with males in federal parliament (Feminist Party of Canada, Statement, 1979). I think I am not being impatient in expressing the sentiment that 842 years is at least 840 years too long!

Other mistaken perceptions of change in women's roles are not difficult to find and in each case the issue at stake has always been power. Rita McWilliams-Tullberg in her study 'Women and degrees at Cambridge University, 1862–1897' points out that the controversy surrounding women's admittance to universities as scholars and members was not really about access to education but about access to power. She notes that

> it was not until 1948 that women were admitted to university membership. By then the voting rights of non-resident graduates had been reduced to a token and the number of women residents at Cambridge was contained at a reassuringly low level. (McWilliams-Tullberg, 1977, p. 120)

Within the medical profession in America, Judith Lorber (1975) shows, women, although they obviously anticipated otherwise, were disadvantaged by their acceptance into co-educational medical schools. The female medical schools to which they had belonged and which had allowed them full participation in affiliated women's hospitals were closed. Their quota in the co-educational schools was restricted to 5 per cent and they had to compete directly with their male colleagues for appointments in hospitals where they often were passed over in favour of male students.

Lorber also identifies women's structural exclusion from the highest ranks of status and power within the medical profession through a form of gatekeeping, not unlike the one employed in the publishing industry. She refers to a 'system of professional patronage and sponsorship which tracked them [women] out of the prestigious specialties and "inner fraternities" of American medical institutions. . . .' (Lorber, 1975, p. 82). In the 5 per cent quota system and the operation of the 'old-boys network', there is evidence that the barriers to women's entry to the male medical schools were only dropped when men were sure that other controls were working effectively. Not surprisingly, one of the other controls was embodied in male control over publication in medical journals. As in all academic disciplines this was and is of prime importance in achieving a reputation in the field and provided another means of keeping women in their proper place.

If women saw their entrance to male medical schools as a form of progress, they were no more misguided than the women who saw the visible feminist movement in England between 1880 and 1920 as a reflection of women's permanently improved status. The movement, which produced feminist networks, presses, bookshops and even a women's bank (Sarah, 1980), proved to be only temporary. Perhaps it was even mistakenly permitted. Certainly the cry of patriotism that accompanied the First World War and the quick realignment of women behind their men managed to destroy the women's networks that had been established. Today there is so little evidence of the movement and of the 'woman question' that was so passionately debated at the time that most women are surprised to learn of their existence. In spite of the fact that the Fawcett Library in London contains an enormous collection of weekly newpapers, periodicals and publications associated with 'first wave feminism' (Sarah, 1980), feminism is not given much significance in recorded history – if, indeed, it is mentioned at all. Most of the records that relate to a strong feminist movement lie side by side with the 'lost' women writers in private collections and are protected (from whom, one may ask) under lock and key in libraries. There they are fairly safe from harm and very safe from wide recognition. Not for them the repeated consultation by students for use in research; not for them a validation through footnotes or allusion in discussion and debate. Instead, theirs is a passive existence, where they remain silent, unthreatening and relegated, like women, to their 'proper' place.

So the existence of a strong feminist movement today does not necessarily mean, as some of us have dared to hope, that feminism is gaining ground as a world view or a way of life. It can be arbitrarily terminated as it was before. While men control society, they are at liberty to value their privileges more highly than the attainment of an egalitarian society. They can at any time and for any 'honourable' reason – like war – interrupt the operation of feminist networks through print and prevent their growth. They may be happy to tolerate our existence while we do not challenge their 75 to 80 per cent of the market. But history warns us that any threat to the fundamental balance of power in men's favour provokes reaction from those who have most to lose.

Similarly, the movement of a few avowed or undercover feminists into the commercial publishing world and into positions previously reserved for men does not indicate that women are now accepted on equal terms with men. Such movement is more likely to signify that a few feminist women have so far managed not to upset a few influential men or it may be no more than another example of the technique that permits acceptance of the few in order to reject the many. Their presence may be evidence of the now traditional token gesture to keep women quiet.

There is also another very pertinent factor that must be considered. Even if women were given half of the gate-keeping roles in publishing but all else remained the same, it might make no difference at all to the present balance of power. Women are, after all, more than half of the population but their numbers alone do not ensure their access to policy-making and power.

Although women's studies, women writers and women's history seem to be enjoying increased interest, there is no guarantee that this signals a permanent change in the values and interests of society generally. The power to decide how long women's issues remain a 'topic' still remains with men. The 'bandwagon' on to which commercial publishers have jumped may have artificially inflated what we see as real growth in the demand for feminist material. The fact that men now 'own' much of women's work may, in the not too distant future, prove to be a loss rather than a gain. June Arnold says that 'The words of earlier feminists were lost because they were the property of male publishers who easily avoided reprinting them' (1976, p. 19).

There is also a danger associated with the popularity of women's studies in the possibility of the body of knowledge women have created becoming 'objectified' as an academic discipline and incorporated into an established structure. As such it will probably become part of the promotional, hier-archical scheme. It can be (and already is) taught by men who will no doubt move to the top of the ladder. Women will be left, as social expectations dictate, at the lower levels with minimal influence on shaping what might become a male-controlled discipline.

Also, it has recently been pointed out to me that a great deal of women's literature is being published in fairly cheap paperback editions and without a run of well-bound cloth editions. The long-range predictions for this material remaining in circulation come up – negative! Because so many women share their books and because the paper and the binding are not of the calibre that will easily survive the test of time, it is quite reasonable to assume that these editions might fall apart even before feminism is again seen by publishers as passé. It would be ironical but not altogether surprising to find that in fifty years time, the only books from the 1980s that had survived were the expensive and presti-gious cloth-bound editions of man-made information.

Even more significant, in terms of the information in this book, is the possibility that the feminist movement and its close association with print have been allowed to re-emerge because they do not currently present a threat to male power. If, as present trends indicate, print is being replaced as the primary form of communication, then gatekeeping over print can be relaxed and controls can be moved to protect the new areas of power.

The trends that give rise to this sort of speculation are visible in several areas. Firstly, paper is becoming scarce and expensive. In one of a series of articles on women in the year 2000, Jane Trahey suggests 'Perhaps paper will be so rare, so expensive, the publishers will have to find a new way to publish, or they will perish' (1974, p. 61). An obvious result of a paper scarcity is books in print becoming a commodity available to relatively few and if this is the case, then commercial interests will dictate that publishers exploit every possible market to win the few readers who will be able to afford books – even if they are women and the material is feminist. Promotion of feminist material under these circum-stances does not present a major threat to the established male ideology.

We are already seeing, at a time when feminists are moving more surely into print, that general literacy levels are falling. For several years, reports of decreasing literacy among school, college and university students have been issued and the term 'functional illiteracy' has been coined to describe numbers of people who emerge from our educational systems unable to read and write effectively. The implications of this may be that many of the people for whom feminist material offers new and relevant understandings will be unable to make use of it. This constitutes a very effective control over the spread of feminist knowledge.

Even as a form of entertainment, print does not have the same appeal today that it had in the past. For a large proportion of people, television, radio and film have taken over from print as entertainment and leisure activities and have undermined the value of reading and writing skills. The ability to use print is no longer essential for the maintenance of social and family communication. My own children could make-long distance telephone calls long before they could write or read letters. With each generation growing up in an environment where the printed word seems less attractive and less efficient as a form of entertainment or communication, there is a little less pressure to control its form and its feminist content.

The printed word is also being challenged in its role as primary source and recorder of information and knowledge. As our society becomes increasingly oriented towards science and technology, computers and other hardware are acquiring the status previously accorded to print. With their vast capacity to store, compare, extrapolate and predict, computers provide an efficient method of recording information and of programming future development. Information in print that once took years to accumulate and arrange into meaningful patterns can now be provided literally at the press of a button. Sophisticated programmes – already prepared by a new breed of experts, in languages that are totally unfamiliar to the general population – are readily available as 'software' for policy and decision-makers to analyse past performance and plot future directions. A whole new mystique is developing around science and technology while ordinary mortals and conventional print are moving further and further away from what promise to be the new centres of power.

Now I have no objection to the demise of a publishing industry that has consistently used its power to devalue me as a woman and to eclipse the knowledge named by so many women before me. But I have many objections and grave fears about a present and a future in which power, still in men's hands, is again moving to an area and a position where it is inaccessible to women. Just as the publishing mystique served to exclude any who were not members of the dominant group, so are science and technology establishing patterns where all but the selected few are without access or redress to the instant 'programmes' that will dictate our lives in the future. It is entirely possible that we will be excluded from representation in the organization and administration of a society based on the new technologies as surely as we have been while it has been based on print.

There is nothing new to feminists in the observation that educational and other requirements for admittance to positions of power have been set up to exclude women. When classical languages and literature were considered essential for a 'proper' education, women were not given the opportunity to study them. For various reasons, women could not *do* languages. Now in the twentieth century, when science and technology are providing the bases for decision-making, women are showing great aptitude for languages but cannot *do* science and maths.

Women's aptitudes have not miraculously altered. The change that has taken place has been the rearranging of women's prescribed roles in order to accommodate men's chosen roles. As Dale Spender has told us, 'the under-achievement lies not in the girls but in those who do not wish to accept them as equals' (Spender, 1980a p. 130).

Today women are being allowed to enter the new structures at lower levels just as they have been in publishing. They are allowed to operate the new radiation emitting machines (visual display terminals) and are encouraged to feel grateful for still being employed as rumour has it that women's traditional occupations in the clerical sphere will be reduced by technological developments in the area of 40 to 60 per cent. There is of course no rumour or prediction that this 'progress' will create alternative jobs for women to fill. As has always been the case, decisions about implementing new technology have been made by men without considering or consulting women.

The inevitable result is that 'progress' is progress only for men. Women have to meet their needs however and wherever they can. Rita Arditti demonstrates that they will not be met in science where men fill the top jobs, earn the most money, receive most of the research grants and make the important decisions (1980, p. 358). It is not likely that their needs, as women perceive them, will be readily met in any area where men will be required to relinquish some of their traditionally occupied space.

The scenario is familiar – except for the new dimension supplied by feminist understandings of the purposeful, political nature of social arrangements and by our awareness that sisterhood can indeed be powerful. With these insights we would be foolish to accept the growth of women's knowledge and networks in print, however valuable they are to us as women, as an unmitigated sign of women's increased power. We would be equally foolish to stand by and watch men take over management of the new technological society and explain it as 'natural' or inevitable. While we are busy building our knowledge in print, worrying about getting it 'right' and congratulating ourselves when we do, the changes in the balance of power to which we are committed may be moving us further away than ever from an egalitarian society.

Men have proved that they are not prepared to move over unless pressure is applied and for both the women who have gone before and for those who are to follow, our commitment must be to create that pressure. We must insist on making our existence as problematic for men as theirs has been for us. We must take every opportunity to expose and deconstruct political gatekeeping in *all* its forms – whether in the selection of personnel and material within publishing or in the selection of programmers and programmes for computers. Now that we know *how* and *why* our exclusion from the literary culture has been arranged, it would be tragic if in ten years time we were collecting data to document our exclusion from the technological culture.

The idea of an *unprogrammed heritage* of women's lives and truths is far too painful to contemplate!

Chapter 9

Postscript

It is now over two years since I began the work on this book in the area of women and publishing. During that time a number of other women writers have addressed similar problems and certainly the idea of 'gatekeeping' has become a familiar one within feminist circles. Unfortunately, however, the attitude of mainstream publishers and editors does not seem to have been modified, or even challenged by the range of understandings that women have presented. As I discovered two years ago, new insights and 'knowledge' appeal to commercial publishers only when there is mileage to be had and not when serious issues are being raised.

Recently, in Australia, I was approached by a journalist at one of the more serious weekend publications to write an article about the sorts of obstacles that women face in terms of having their work published. Success! A breakthrough! A chance to actually present some feminist understandings to a general, rather than an already committed feminist audience. I was careful to make the article amusing, a little facetious – all of those characteristics that must be allowed for in presenting material to a weekend audience. I made an effort to complete the article quickly and efficiently to show that women writers are serious; I was careful to balance my observations and to allude to studies already completed in the area in order to conform to the notion of credibility. I did not at the time realize the irony of submitting an article to the commercial press in which I set out very clearly all the reasons why such presses rarely publish women's work when it deals with women's, rather than men's understandings.

Need I say more? The article was returned, promptly, with the comment that it was 'not suitable' for the particular publication to which I had sent it (and which had requested the article). The reason provided was that the main allegations were not substantiated with examples ... perhaps I should be grateful that I was at least given an alternative to the 'it has been done before' excuse with which the article specifically dealt!

I have included the article in this postscript as a demonstration of the thesis of the book. The final paragraph of the article states:

> While ever the publishing industry does not have to confront that percentage (one woman published to every five males) as an issue of sexual politics, it should not be hard for those in decision-making positions to ensure that the safe 1:5 ration is maintained.

It would seem that, at this stage, commercial publishers are as committed to keeping that ratio as feminists are to changing it. The odds though, are with the publishers.

Politics in Publishing?

Have you noticed how stoically the publishing industry resists the temptation to reply to critics who accuse it of partiality or poor judgment? Indeed, have you noticed how the publishing industry rarely, if ever, enters into public debate about its principles and practices? Certainly, from time to time, we hear of the terrible financial problems, the increasing costs, the removal or granting of various subsidies, but never do we actually hear anything about who makes the decisions relating to the selection of material for publication. Nor, might I add, do we ever hear on what basis those decisions are made.

It is surprising in an institution which probably has as much influence in establishing the boundaries of our intellectual lives as do governments in establishing the boundaries of our ideological lives, that there is so little notion of accountability to the people to whom its decisions are relevant. Perhaps the publishing industry is seen as sufficiently removed from the centres of power for its values to be assumed to be impartial. Whatever the explanation, there is no systematic monitoring of the publishing industry in terms of its selection of particular 'private' ideas and images for 'public' circulation. There are no courses on this aspect of publishing that are readily available in schools, colleges or universities. There is no regular forum (outside the industry) where discussion and debate are encouraged. It is almost as if the publishing industry deliberately discouraged public scrutiny and actively promoted a mystique designed to repel the attention of outsiders. Questions directed at publishers about their decision-making processes tend to be answered with references to marketability, the economic climate and a vague and elusive notion of 'standards'. It would seem that the one thing that publishers do not wish to make public is the rationale for their own activities.

This reticence could be attributable to a jealous guarding of information in what is a very competitive arena; it could be attributable to the fact that publishers themselves do not really know on what basis they make their decisions. There is a belief among the publishing moguls that 'flair' – a sense of smell – is the essential quality for a successful publisher, but were that really the case, the popular image of the publisher would not be of the erudite scholar and gentleman poring over manuscripts in search of new knowledge and new literary talent. Instead the image would be of a Sherlock Holmes-type, sniffing his way around writers in the hope that he might detect the particular odour that signals success. However, as neither of these images really reflects the activities of publishers and as few publishers ever pay more than passing attention to unsolicited manuscripts (one publisher I know uses a bundle of manuscripts as a door-stop and another made them his contribution to the energy crisis by using them as fuel), then there must be an alternative explanation. Is it just possible that publishers and editors encourage the notion of there being some specific, but unnamed, rationale involved in publishing decision-making so that while writers scurry around their desks and typewriters writing and re-writing in order to 'crack the code', publishers are sending their secretaries to their desks to type up contracts for the already commissioned books and articles that it suits them to publish?

If this is the case, then there are dimensions to publishing decision-making that should come into the open for public discussion. Whose interests are being served? While few would argue that within commercial publishing, the profits of the company are of primary importance, there may also be a political element involved. If available figures are correct (and in spite of the fact that few of the men involved in writing and publishing seem to agree) there may be a genuine case of sexual politics – at women's expense – lying dormant behind the closed doors of the publishing industry.

In the nineteenth century when men were complaining that the literary profession was being invaded by 'women, children and ill-trained troops', studies show that the ratio of women to men in terms of published work stood at about 1:5, or close to 20 per cent. In the last decade, during which men have again complained that women's material has flooded the market, the ratio has remained relatively unchanged and as Elaine Showalter reminds us in her book about women novelists, 'The same complaints [have] been made since 1771; it is important to realize that "female dominance" is always in the eye of the male beholder'. The real change has been one in women's visibility and men's consciousness rather than a change in publishing practice. The fact that men have noticed – and resented – women constituting 20 per cent of published writers only makes sense if they think that women should not be there at all. Rather, they should be noticing that women, as over half the population and with access to what men assure us are equal educational and career oppor-tunities, do not make up 52 per cent of the current literary producers.

Publishers, from what I can gather, think that material about women and by women (that is, 'political' writing) is finite. Presumably such material has a beginning and an end and by all accounts should reach saturation point within a certain period of time. On the other hand, material about men and by men (that is, anything written from a male perspective and which women could see as 'political') is not considered to have a limited life-span or limited interest value. When a downturn in the demand for men's material is felt, it is assumed to be connected with general economic conditions while a similar downturn in women's material is perceived as the inevitable demise of a current trend. As a result, what has happened in the past and may well happen again, is that women's material goes 'out of print'. Just at the time when it seems that women's material might indeed break through the 1:5 ratio, the fad is said to be over, the normal ratio is maintained and the literary men breathe a sigh of relief and retreat behind their closed doors. Convenient, isn't it?

I do not know whether publishers are genuinely convinced that, after all, only so much can be said by women about women, or whether their 'flair' tells them that women's material is beginning to acquire the wrong scent. I do know that if a woman writer can have an article on women and sport rejected because it has been 'done before' while articles about men and sport appear daily in all sorts of publications, then publishers can justifiably be accused of playing sexual politics. Under these circumstances it is not difficult to see the publishing mystique as a convenient means of avoiding public recognition that 80 per cent of the material produced in our society has shown a consistently masculist bias. While ever the publishing industry does not have to confront that percentage as an issue of sexual politics, it should not be too hard for those in the decision-making positions to ensure that the safe 1:5 ratio is maintained and that we continue to be presented with a predominantly male view of the world until well into the twenty-first century.

Notes to Transcripts

For obvious reasons, only a general context is given for each of the quoted comments.

1 Published writer, USA, correspondence, 1980.
2 Documentation for Women's Research and Resources Centre seminar, 'Women and Writing', London, February 1979
3 Ibid.
4 Ibid.
5 Published writer, Canada, interview, 1980.
6 Published writer, USA, interview, 1981.
7 Published writer, Canada, interview, 1981.
8 Published writer, Canada, discussion, 1980.
9 Unpublished writer, Canada, discussion, 1980.
10 Published writer, USA, correspondence, 1980.
11 Published writer, England, correspondence, 1980.
12 Published writer, England, correspondence, 1980.
13 Published writer, England, correspondence, 1980.
14 Published writer, USA, discussion, 1980.
15 Published writer, England, newspaper article, 1979.
16 Published writer, Canada, interview, 1980.
17 Published writer, England, correspondence, 1980.
18 Correspondence between editor and writer, England, 1980.
19 Published writer, England, interview, 1980.
20 Published writer, England, correspondence, 1980.
21 Published writer, USA, correspondence, 1980.
22 Newspaper article, England, 1980.
23 Editor, general publishing house, Canada, 1980.

24 Editor, academic publishing house, Canada, 1980.
25 Editor, general publishing house, Canada, 1980.
26 Editor, general publishing house, England, 1980.
27 Editor, educational publishing house, Canada, 1980.
28 Editor, general publishing house, Canada, 1980.
29 Editor, general publishing house, Canada, 1980.
30 Editor, general publishing house, USA, 1980.
31 Editor/writer, general publishing house, USA, 1980.
32 Editor/writer, newspaper, Canada, 1980.
33 Editorial Assistant, general publishing house, USA, 1980.
34 Editor, trade publisher, England, 1980.
35 Designer/publisher, self-employed, Australia, 1982.
36 Editor, freelance, Australia, 1982.
37 Editor, general publishing house, Canada, 1980.
38 Editor, general publishing house, England, 1980.
39 Editor, general publishing house, Canada, 1980.
40 Editor, general publishing house, Canada, 1980.
41 Editor, general publishing house, England, 1980.
42 Editor, general publishing house, Canada, 1980.
43 Editor, general publishing house, USA, 1980.
44 Editor, general publishing house, England, 1980.
45 Editorial assistant, general publishing house, Canada, 1980.
46 Editor, commercial publishing house, England, 1980.
47 Editor, commercial publishing house, England, 1980.
48 Editor, feminist publishing house, USA, 1980.
49 Editor, feminist publishing house, Canada, 1980.
50 Editor, general publishing house, England, 1980.
51 Editor, feminist publishing house, USA, 1980.
52 Editor, general publishing house, England, 1980.
53 Editor, feminist publishing house, Canada, 1980.

Bibliography

Applebaum, Judith and **Evans, Nancy** (1978), *How To Get Happily Published*, Harper & Row, New York.

Arditti, Rita (1980), 'Feminism and science', in Rita Arditti, Pat Brennan and Steve Cavrack (eds), *Science and Liberation*, Black Rose Books, Montreal.

Arnold, June (1976), 'Feminist presses and feminist politics', *Quest: A Feminist Quarterly*, 3, no. 1, summer, pp. 18–26.

Armstrong, Dr Scott (1980), in Michael Leapman, 'Diary of impermeable prose', *The Times*, 9 June, p. 14.

Backhouse, Constance and **Cohen, Leah** (1978), *The Secret Oppression*, Macmillan of Canada.

Baehr, Helen (1980), 'The "liberated woman" in television drama', *Women's Studies International Quarterly*, 3, no., 1, pp. 29–39.

Baron, Martin J. (1980), 'On Vanity Publishing', in Bill Henderson (ed.), *The Publish-it-Yourself Handbook*, Pushcart Press, Yonkers, New York, pp. 49–55.

Batt, Sharon (1980), 'Feminist publishing: where small is not so beautiful', *Status of Women, Canada News*, 6, no. 2, Spring, pp. 12–13.

Beasley, Maureen and **Gibbons, Sheila** (eds) (1977), *Women in Media: A Documentary Source Book*, Women's Institute for Freedom of the Press, Washington, D.C.

de Beauvoir, Simone (1972), *The Second Sex*, Penguin, Harmondsworth.

Bernikow, Louise (ed.) (1974), *The World Split Open: Four Centuries of Women Poets in England and America, 1552–1950*, Vintage, New York.

Byrne, Eileen (1978), *Women and Education*, Tavistock, London.

Callil, Carmen (1981), in Polly Toynbee, 'We tend to publish what feels right and then see what it all adds up to afterwards', *The Guardian*, 26 January.

Chesler, Phyllis (1972), *Women and Madness*, Avon Books, New York.

Clausen, Jan (1976), 'The politics of publishing and the lesbian community', *Sinister Wisdom*, 1, no. 2, Fall, pp. 95–115.

Cliff, Michelle (1979), 'The Resonance of interruption', *Chrysalis: a magazine of women's culture*, no. 8, Summer, pp. 29–37.

Daly, Mary (1973), *Beyond God the Father: Toward a philosophy of women's liberation*, Beacon Press, Boston.

Daly, Mary (1978), *Gyn/Ecology: the Metaethics of Radical Feminism*, Beacon Press, Boston.

Deem, Rosemary (ed.) (1980), *Schooling for Women's Work*, Routledge & Kegan Paul, London.

Dixson, Miriam (1976), *The Real Matilda: Woman and Identity in Australia 1788–1975*, Penguin, Harmondsworth.

Dobson, Austin (1903), 'Introduction' to Fanny Burney's *Evelina*, Macmillan & Co, London.

Ehrenreich, Barbara and **English, Deirdre** (1979), *For Her Own Good: 150 Years of the Experts' Advice to Women*, Pluto Press, London.

Ellman, Mary (1968), *Thinking About Women*, Harcourt, Brace Jovanovich, New York.

Evans, Sir Ifor (1963), *A Short History of English Literature*, Penguin, Harmondsworth.

Farley, Lin (1978), *Sexual Shakedown: The Sexual Harassment of Women on the Job*, McGraw-Hill, New York.

Finch, Anne, Countess of Winchelsea (1974), in Joan Goulianos (ed.), *By a Woman Writt*, Penguin, Harmondsworth.

Fuller, Margaret (1971), *Women in the Nineteenth Century*, Norton, New York.

Gelpi, Barbara (1980), in Karen J. Winkler, 'Signs of change in Women's Studies: the success of an Uncommon Journal', *The Chronicle of Higher Education*, 15 September, pp. 23 and 30.

Gilbert, Sandra M. and **Gubar, Susan** (1979), *The Madwoman in the Attic*, Yale University Press, London.

Goldberg, Philip (1974), 'Are women prejudiced against women?', in J. Stacey, S. Beréaud and J. Daniels (eds), *And Jill Came Tumbling After: Sexism in American Education*, Dell, New York, pp. 37–42.

Goreau, Angeline (1980), *Reconstructing Aphra: a Social Biography of Aphra Behn*, Dial Press, New York.

Gornick, Vivian and **Moran, Barbara K.** (eds) (1971), *Woman in Sexist Society: Studies in Power and Powerlessness*, Basic Books, New York.

Gould, Lois (1977), 'Creating a women's world', *The New York Times Magazine*, 2 January, p. 11.

Goulianos, Joan (ed.) (1974), *By a Woman Writt: Literature from Six Centuries by and about Women*, Penguin, Harmondsworth.

Govier, Katherine (1979), 'Coach house and women's press . . . staying small and thriving', *Quill and Quire*, Canada, July, pp. 15–16.

Greer, Germaine (1974), 'Flying pigs and double standards', *Times Literary Supplement*, London, 26 July, pp. 784–5.

Greer, Germaine (1979), *The Obstacle Race*, Secker & Warburg, London.

Grimstad, Kirsten (1979), 'The state of the art', in Linda Palumbo, Feminist Publishing Catalogue, *Chrysalis*, no. 8, Summer, pp. 105–8.

Harms, Valerie (1979), 'Interview: Valerie Harms', Sharon Spencer, *Motheroot Journal*, Spring, p. 2.

Haskell, Molly (1974), in Jane Trahey, 'The female facade: fierce, fragile and fading', in Maggie Tripp (ed.), *Woman in the Year 2000*, Dell, New York.

Heller, John S. and **Robin, M.** (1974), *The Physician and Sexuality in Victorian America*, University of Illinois Press.

Henderson, Bill (ed.) (1980), *The Publish-it-Yourself Handbook, Literary Tradition and How-to*, Pushcart Press, Yonkers, New York.

Hess, Thomas B. and **Baker, Elizabeth C.** (1975), *Art and Sexual Politics*, Collier-Macmillan, London.

Hubbard, Ruth (1979), 'Reflections on the story of the double helix', *Women's Studies International Quarterly*, 2, no. 3, pp. 261–7.

Janeway, Elizabeth (1980), *Powers of the Weak*, Knopf, New York.

Joan, Polly and **Chesman, Andrea** (1978), *Guide to Women's Publishing*, Dustbooks, Paradise, California.

Kamm, Josephine (1966), *Rapiers and Battleaxes*, Allen & Unwin, London.

Kaplan, Cora (1978), 'Introduction' to *Aurora Leigh and other Poems: Elizabeth Barrett Browning*, The Women's Press, pp. 5–36.

Kramnick, Miriam (ed.) (1975), *Wollstonecraft: Vindication of the Rights of Woman*, Penguin, Harmondsworth.

Kuhn, Thomas S. (1970) (2nd edn), *The Structure of Scientific Revolutions*, University of Chicago Press.

Leapman, Michael (1980), 'Diary of impermeable prose', *The Times*, 9 June, p. 14.

Lewis, Jane (1981), 'History', in Dale Spender (ed.), *Men's Studies Modified*, Pergamon Press, Oxford.

Lorber, Judith (1975), 'Women and medical sociology: invisible professionals and ubiquitous patients', in Marcia Millman and Rosabeth Moss Kanter (eds), *Another Voice: Feminist Perspectives* on Social Life and Social Science, Anchor Books, Doubleday, New York, pp. 75–105.

McWilliams-Tullberg, Rita (1977), 'Women and degrees at Cambridge, 1862–1897', in Martha Vicinus (ed.), *A Widening Sphere: Changing Roles of Victorian Women*, Indiana University Press, pp. 117–45.

Maeroff, Gene (1979), 'Journals' problem: what to publish?', *New York Times*, 14 August, pp. C1 and C4.

Mahl, Mary R. and **Koon, Helene** (eds) (1979), *The Female Spectator*, The Feminist Press, New York.

Manley, Seon and **Belcher, Susan** (1972), *O, Those Extraordinary Women! or the joys of literary lib*, Chilton, Philadelphia.

Marcus, Jane (1980), 'Introduction', in Elizabeth Robins, *The Convert*, The Women's Press, London.

Mill, John Stuart (1974), 'The subjection of women', in Alice S. Rossi (ed.), *The Feminist Papers: From Adams to de Beauvoir*, Bantam, New York, pp. 196–238.

Miller, Casey and **Swift, Kate** (1977), *Words and Women*, Doubleday, New York.

Miller, Jean Baker (1977), *Towards a New Psychology of Women*, Beacon Press, Boston.

Millett, Kate (1971), *Sexual Politics*, Sphere Books, London.

Millman, Marcia and **Moss Kanter, Rosabeth** (eds) (1975), *Another Voice: Feminist Perspectives on Social Life and Social Change*, Anchor Press/Doubleday, New York.

Mitchell, Juliet and **Oakley, Ann** (eds) (1976), *The Rights and Wrongs of Women*, Penguin, Harmondsworth.

Modjeska, Drusilla (1981), *Exiles at Home: Australian Women Writers 1925–1945*, Angus & Robertson, Australia.

Moers, Ellen (1977), *Literary Women*, Anchor Press/Doubleday, New York.

Morgan, Elaine (1979), 'Writing for television: women's contribution', *Women's Studies International Quarterly*, 2, no. 2, pp. 209–13.

Nin, Anaïs (1980), 'The story of my printing press', in Henderson, Bill (ed.), *The Publish-it-Yourself Handbook*, Pushcart, pp. 29–32.

Nochlin, Linda (1971), 'Why are there no great women artists?' in Vivian Gornick and Barbara K. Moran (eds), *Woman in Sexist Society: Studies in Power and Powerlessness*', Basic Books, New York, pp. 480–510.

Oakley, Ann (1974), *Housewife*, Allen Lane, London; (1976), Penguin, Harmondsworth.

Olsen, Tillie (1979), *Silences*, Delta, New York.

Petesch, Natalie (1979), in 'Life piled on life: an interview with Natalie Petesch', Patricia Schweitzer, *Motheroot Journal*, Winter, pp. 1 and 7.

Rich, Adrienne (1979), *On Lies, Secrets and Silences: Selected Prose 1966–78*, Norton, New York.

Roberts, Helen (1981a), 'Sociology', in Dale Spender (ed.), *Men's Studies Modified*, Pergamon Press, Oxford.

Roberts, Helen (1981b), *Doing Feminist Research*, Routledge & Kegan Paul, London.

Roberts, Joan I. (1976), *Beyond Intellectual Sexism: A New Woman, a New Reality*, David McKay, New York.

Rogers, Katharine M. (1968), *The Troublesome Helpmate: A History of Misogyny in Literature*, University of Washington Press.

Rogers, Katharine M. (ed.) (1979), *Before Their Time*, Frederick Ungar, New York.

Rooney, Frances (1980), 'Our names in print', *Canadian Women's Studies*, II, no. 2, pp. 21–2.

Rossi, Alice S. (ed.) (1974), *The Feminist Papers: from Adams to Beauvoir*, Bantam, New York.

Ruddick, Sara and **Daniels, Pamela** (eds) (1977), *Working it Out*, Pantheon, New York.

Sachs, Albie and **Hoff Wilson, Joan** (1978), *Sexism and the Law*, Martin Robertson, Oxford.

Sarah, Elizabeth (1980), paper on 'first-wave feminism' given at Women's Research and Resources Centre conference, 'Women's Liberation Movement and Men', London, 23 March.

Showalter, Elaine (1971), 'Women writers and the double standard', in Vivian Gornick and Barbara K. Moran (eds), *Woman in Sexist Society*, Basic Books, New York, pp. 452–79.

Showalter, Elaine (1978), *A Literature of their Own: British Women Novelists from Brontë to Lessing*, Virago, London.

Smith, Dorothy (1978), 'A peculiar eclipsing: women's exclusion from man's culture', *Women's Studies International Quarterly* 1, no. 4, pp. 281–96.

Spacks, Patricia Meyer (1976), *The Female Imagination*, Avon, New York.

Spender, Dale (1980a), in Dale Spender and Elizabeth Sarah (eds), *Learning to Lose: Sexism and Education*, The Women's Press, London.

Spender, Dale (1980b), *Man Made Language*, Routledge & Kegan Paul, London.

Spender, Dale (1981a), 'The gatekeepers: a feminist critique of academic publishing', in Helen Roberts (ed.), *Doing Feminist Research*, Routledge & Kegan Paul, London, pp. 186–202.

Spender, Dale (1981b), *Men's Studies Modified: The Impact of Feminism on the Academic Disciplines*, Pergamon Press, Oxford.

Spender, Dale (1982a), *Women of Ideas – and what men have done* *to them: from Aphra Behn to Adrienne Rich*, Routledge & Kegan Paul, London.

Spender, Dale (1982b), *Invisible Women: the Schooling Scandal*, Writers' and Readers' Publishing Co-operative, London.

Stacey, Judith, Béreaud, Susan and **Daniels, Joan** (eds) (1974), *And Jill Came Tumbling After: Sexism in American Education*, Dell, New York.

Stanton, Elizabeth Cody, and the Revising Committee, 1974, (6th printing 1978), *The Woman's Bible*, Coalition Task Force on Women and Religion, Seattle.

Strainchamps, Ethel (ed.) (1974), *Rooms with no View: A Woman's Guide to the Man's World of the Media*, Harper & Row, New York.

Stubbs, Patricia (1981), *Women and Fiction: Feminism and the Novel 1880–1920*, Methuen, London.

Trahey, Jane (1974), 'The female facade: fierce, fragile and fading', in Maggie Tripp (ed.), *Woman in the Year 2000*, Dell, New York, pp. 54–67.

Unwin, Sir Stanley (1960, 7th edn), *The Truth About Publishing*, Allen & Unwin, London.

Vicinus, Martha (ed.) (1977), *A Widening Sphere: Changing Roles of Victorian Women*, Indiana University Press.

West, Celeste and **Wheat, Valerie** (1978), *The Passionate Perils of Publishing*, Booklegger, San Franciso.

Wolfe, Margie (1980), 'Feminist publishing in Canada', *Canadian Women's Studies*, II, no. 2, pp. 11–14.

Wolfe, Morris (1975), 'Of Ms and Men in Publishing', *Books in Canada*, May, pp. 4–6.

Woolf, Virginia (1977a), *A Room of One's Own*, Granada, England.

Woolf, Virginia (1977b), *Three Guineas*, The Hogarth Press, London.

Woolf, Virginia (1979), *Women and Writing*, The Women's Press, London.

Zimet, Sara Goodman (1977), *Print and Prejudice*, Hodder & Stoughton, London.

Index